Tom Fallers—
with warmest Regards
Dan

Marriage, Authority,

AND

Final Causes

A STUDY OF UNILATERAL CROSS-COUSIN MARRIAGE

By George C. Homans
and David M. Schneider

THE FREE PRESS, GLENCOE, ILLINOIS

THIS IS a study of a rare phenomenon that provides a crucial test of theory. Preferential marriage is the familiar fact that in many societies ego, besides being forbidden to marry certain women, is expected to marry one or more of a class of women standing in certain kin relationships to him. Among the forms of preferential marriage, unilateral cross-cousin marriage exists when, as between his two female cross-cousins, ego male is expected to marry one but not the other: his mother's brother's daughter but not his father's sister's daughter or *vice-versa*. Only a handful of societies follow such a rule: it is much less common than most of the other rules of preferential marriage. Unilateral cross-cousin marriage gets its interest from the fact that, perhaps just because it occurs only under special conditions, a study of what determines the adoption by a society of one rather than the other of its forms allows us to compare the usefulness of a final-cause theory with that of an efficient-cause theory of social behavior. We give the theories these names for want of better ones. The final-cause theory is in fact the one presented by Claude Lévi-Strauss in his book *Les structures élémentaires de la parenté*.[1] Whatever its title may imply, this is not a study of kinship behavior in general but of preferential marriage. The efficient-cause theory derives ultimately from A. R. Radcliffe-Brown's classic paper, "The Mother's Brother in South Africa."[2]

Introduction to Lévi-Strauss's argument

Lévi-Strauss examines several forms of preferential marriage besides the unilateral cross-cousin one, and to bring out the nature of his theory we must begin with what he has to say about these other forms.[3] He starts from the assumption that marrying and giving in marriage are processes of exchanging perhaps the most highly valued of scarce goods, to wit: women. If my group gives its sisters and daughters to the men of another group, it must have some means of recouping its losses: it must get women back. Indeed he links the incest prohibition itself to preferential mating: "The prohibition of the sexual usage of the daughter or the sister requires that the daughter or sister be given to some other man, and at the same time it creates a right over the daughter or sister of the other man."[4] He goes even further, and this is the first hint of his final-cause interpretation of marriage rules, saying that the incest taboo is set up *in order that* an exchange may take place. His words are: "The content of the [incest] prohibition is not exhausted by the fact of the prohibition; the latter is instituted only to found and guarantee, directly or indirectly, immediately or mediately, an exchange."[5] Note this well: he is not saying that the incest taboo and other marriage rules in fact produce exchanges of women between groups of men, but that the rules exist *because* they produce the exchanges. We shall see later why he thinks the exchanges so important.

In societies where membership in groups is defined by descent, a rule prescribing marriage with a parallel cousin hardly creates any exchange of women between groups. You are giving your women to, and getting them from, members of your own lineage. Such a rule is very rare:[6] Lévi-Strauss would say because it failed to produce exchange. The division of a tribe into un-ilineally-defined moieties, with the rule that ego must marry a woman of the moiety other than his own, automatically turns a parallel cousin into a prohibited spouse and creates the exchange of women between groups. At this point Lévi-Strauss undertakes the study of the various forms of cross-cousin marriage, beginning with the classic Australian systems: Kariera, Aranda, Murngin, etc. His book makes clear as few others do how these rules work, and his exposition is often magnificent. This is one of the great ethnographic summaries. In differing from Lévi-

Strauss at certain points, we shall never deny that his book is a most distinguished one—partly because its argument is clear enough to *make* us disagree.

Restricted and generalized exchange

Among the Kariera, ego is expected to marry mother's brother's daughter *or* father's sister's daughter. That is, the rules for a man and for a woman are the same: each may marry either cross-cousin. This is a form of *bilateral* cross-cousin marriage. The ideal is that a brother and sister should marry a sister and brother and that, in the next generation, ego should marry mother's brother's daughter who is at the same time father's sister's daughter. In any event, kin groups (usually called *sections*) in the society are paired, and they swap women. For this reason Lévi-Strauss calls the system *restricted exchange*. The Kariera have four sections. In other systems, such as the Aranda, the number of sections may increase by powers of two, and ego may marry, not his immediate cross-cousin, but some more distant one. Yet the characteristic of restricted exchange—pairs of sections that swap women—is preserved. Without this characteristic, it is doubtful that Lévi-Strauss would give the name *restricted exchange* to a rule simply allowing marriage with either cross-cousin.

As distinguished from bilateral cross-cousin marriage, the unilateral form exists when, as between the two kinds of female cross-cousin—mother's brother's daughter and father's sister's daughter—, the members of the society say that they prefer or expect ego to marry one of the two, but disapprove or at best tolerate his marriage with the other. That is, the rule for a man is different from that for a woman: if a man marries his mother's brother's daughter, a woman marries her father's sister's son. This kind of rule Lévi-Strauss reaches with the Murngin, who want ego to marry mother's brother's daughter but *not* father's sister's daughter. And he spends most of the rest of his book on this, the *matrilateral* form of unilateral cross-cousin marriage, which realizes what he calls *generalized exchange* and admires as a step forward in human marriage arrangements. Preferred marriage with father's sister's daughter but *not* mother's brother's daughter is the *patrilateral* form of unilateral cross-cousin marriage. Because Lévi-Strauss himself lays so much weight on these rules we make them the focus of our criticism of his theory.

Lévi-Strauss is always interested in the formal properties of the social structure associated with a marriage norm. Thus he must neglect the degree to which natives depart from the norm in practice, and depart from it they must. If, among the Kariera, for instance, the number of marriageable, true, female cross-cousins does not equal the number of marriageable, true, male cross-cousins—and this must almost always be the case—, the ideal system cannot be carried out, and the men will marry classificatory cross-cousins. Although this will be true to some degree of all marriage rules, Lévi-Strauss always deals with the ideal system, and for purposes of argument we shall follow him.

Let us now look at the structural properties of matrilateral cross-cousin marriage, strictly carried out. Lévi-Strauss can easily show (see Figure 1) that, given mother's brother's daughter marriage and either patrilineal or matrilineal descent groups (lineages), the groups in question must be at least three in number; that is, a simple moiety organization cannot exist. For under the stipulated conditions the men of lineage A marry the women of lineage B, but the men of B do not reciprocate by marrying the women of A, or the system would become one of Kariera type in which marriage with either cross-cousin is allowed. The conditions require instead three lineages, in which the men of A lineage marry B women, the B men marry Cs, and the C men marry As, in a ring. Indeed the ring can be extended to any number of lineages, and for this reason Lévi-Strauss calls the system one of *generalized exchange:* the Bs give women to the As; they do not get women back from the As—that would be restricted exchange—, but they do get women back in a roundabout way from a lineage on the other side of them in the ring. It might be argued that in extending the idea of exchange in this way, Lévi-Strauss has thinned the meaning out of it. Of course some of the tribes following this rule say they exchange women for *goods*, but when Lévi-Strauss talks about marriage exchange he always means the exchange of women for *women*, whether recognized as an exchange or not.

Leaving Australia behind him, Lévi-Strauss goes on to show that, with some variations, the system of generalized exchange, with preferred marriage between ego and mother's brother's daughter, exists or existed in the past in a number of societies extending in a crescent from India through China to eastern Siberia. We know, of course, that this type of marriage occurs in other parts of the world, but Lévi-Strauss chooses to make eastern Asia his area of demonstration, and again his sheer exposition of the marriage rules in this ethnographic area seems excellent.

Harmonic and dysharmonic societies

We now bring up a problem that we should like to avoid but cannot, because it will turn out to have incidental, though only incidental, importance for our argument. Lévi-Strauss makes a further distinction between the bilateral and the unilateral form of cross-cousin marriage. He says the former is associated with *dysharmonic* regimes and the latter with *harmonic* ones.[7] To understand what he means by this we must consider for the first time the rules governing the constitution of the kin-groups that, directly or indirectly, exchange women. Lévi-Strauss says: "We shall call a regime harmonic when the rule of residence is the same as the rule of filiation, dysharmonic when they are different."[8] Thus a patrilocal (residence), patrilineal (filiation) society is harmonic, a patrilocal, matrilineal one dysharmonic. Contrary to usual practice in anthropology, words like *patrilocal* do not refer here to the place of residence of a couple after marriage but to the place of residence of ego in relation to the place of residence of the member of the older generation from whom ego

[7]

inherits lineage membership. Thus if descent is patrilineal, and ego resides in the same local group as his father, the regime, according to Lévi-Strauss, is harmonic.

Consider now an harmonic society of the patrilineal-patrilocal sort. If the marriage rule is bilateral and the society is dichotomized once, so that every person, male or female, has to marry into a moiety other than his own, the moieties being defined either by descent or by residence but not by both, no trouble arises. But if the society is dichotomized twice, so that there are two residence moieties and two descent moieties, and if a person belongs to the same residence moiety and the same descent moiety as his father (that is, the regime is harmonic), and if, finally, he must marry outside both his moieties, the following situation arises:[9]

If a man:	marries a woman:	the children will be:
A1	B2	A1
B2	A1	B2
A2	B1	A2
B1	A2	B1

That is, the society divides into two pairs of sections, in this example A1-B2 and A2-B1. The two members of each pair are linked to one another by marriage, but the pairs themselves are linked neither by marriage nor by descent. The society splits wholly in two.

But if, the other rules remaining the same, ego belongs to the same residence moiety as his father but to a different descent moiety, that is, if the regime becomes, in Lévi-Strauss's terms, matrilineal-patrilocal and thus dysharmonic, then the following situation results:

$$\uparrow A1 = B2 \uparrow \qquad\qquad \text{descent} \longleftrightarrow$$
$$\downarrow A2 = B1 \downarrow \qquad\qquad \text{marriage} =$$

That is, the sections are all linked, two pairs by marriage and two, cross-cutting pairs by descent. This is the Kariera system, which Lévi-Strauss argues is matrilineal, patrilocal. In fact it makes no odds whether we call it that or a system of patrilineal moieties intersected by matrilineal ones or a system of patrilineal moieties further subdivided by alternating generations—the only required condition is that, in a doubly dichotomized society, a person should belong to one of his father's moieties but not the other.

Accordingly Lévi-Strauss argues that dysharmonic societies can go on dichotomizing themselves indefinitely into four, eight, sixteen, etc. sections, still preserving restricted exchange and some form of bilateral marriage rule and still linking all the sections together by marriage or descent as shown above. But harmonic societies cannot dichotomize themselves more than once and accomplish all the rest too. The question then arises: What form of marriage rule can an harmonic society adopt that will automatically link more than two common-residence-and-descent groups (lineages) together? Lévi-Strauss says it can only abandon a bilateral rule and adopt a unilateral one. Then any number of lineages can be linked together in a ring by marriage, as we have already shown for the matrilateral case and will show for the patrilateral one. For these reasons, Lévi-Strauss says, bilateral cross-cousin marriage, at least of the various Australian forms, will be associated with dysharmonic regimes, unilateral cross-cousin marriage with harmonic ones.

Marriage rules and organic solidarity

Why, the reader may well ask, does Lévi-Strauss consider so important the linking together, through marriage, of the different groups within a society? Why do they *have* to be linked? We can best answer this question by trying to answer another one: Why does he consider matrilateral cross-cousin marriage a step forward in human marriage arrangements? The answer is that he holds generalized exchange to be *better* than restricted exchange from the point of view of the organic solidarity of a society. In restricted exchange the number of sections can increase by powers of two, but as far as marriage is concerned, each section is linked with only one other, and the two swap women directly: there is no "roundaboutness"; whereas in generalized exchange each lineage specializes with respect to two others, from one of which it receives women and to the other of which it gives them. What is more, no lineage can get the women it needs unless the whole ring of marriage transactions works correctly. In Lévi-Strauss's view this makes for the closer integration of the tribe. His words are: "In effect, generalized exchange allows, the group remaining the same in extension and composition, the realization, in the heart of this mechanically stable group, of a greater organic solidarity."[10]

Lévi-Strauss is a French social scientist, and the parentage of his theory is clear. In the language of the turf, it is by Émile Durkheim out of Marcel Mauss's *Essai sur le don*. According to Durkheim in *De la division du travail social*,[11] a society is organically solidary to the extent that its individual members or sub-groups are specialists and so dependent on one another, a further implication being that a solidary society is one showing a capacity to maintain itself in the face of disruptive tendencies. While Durkheim is talking for the most part about occupational specialization (the division of labor), Lévi-Strauss is talking about the specialization of one group with respect to others in giving women in marriage, but we believe the two men mean the same thing by *organic solidarity*. For Lévi-Strauss the greater the marriage specialization of each of the kin-groups in a society, the greater the dependence of each upon all, and hence the greater the organic solidarity.

Matrilateral and patrilateral cross-cousin marriage

We now reach the empirical focus of this paper: the two different forms of unilateral cross-cousin marriage. For the reader

MATRILINEAGES

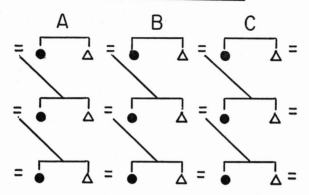

Fig I. Matrilateral Cross-Cousin Marriage (Matrilineal Society).

MATRILINEAGES

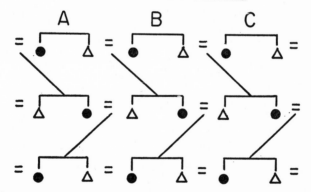

Fig. 2. Patrilateral Cross-Cousin Marriage (Matrilineal Society).

will remember that there are *two*, though up to this point in his argument Lévi-Strauss has considered only one of them. Preferred marriage with mother's brother's daughter but not father's sister's daughter is generalized exchange. But how about preferred marriage with father's sister's daughter and not with the other cross-cousin (the patrilateral form)? Just as Lévi-Strauss argues that, from the point of view of organic solidarity, generalized exchange is better than restricted exchange, so he argues that from the same point of view mother's brother's daughter marriage (generalized exchange) is *better* than father's sister's daughter marriage.

It can readily be shown—and Lévi-Strauss does show—that the formal structure created by the patrilateral form is not just the mirror opposite of that created by the matrilateral one. (Compare figures 1 and 2.) In the latter, the men of B lineage always marry C women—the Cs are "givers of women" with respect to the Bs—, A men always marry B women, and so forth; whereas in the former a B man marries a C woman in one generation, his sister's son marries an A woman in the next, his sister's daughter's son marries a C woman in the third, and so on, the Bs being by alternate generations givers and receivers of women with respect to the As and the Cs. The two systems are structurally different, and the difference holds whether the society is matrilineal, as our figures assume, or patrilineal, son and grandson taking, in the latter case, the place of sister's son and sister's daughter's son in the former.

Lévi-Strauss calls father's sister's daughter marriage *discontinuous exchange.* And he asks, "What does this mean? Instead of constituting a global system, as do both bilateral and matrilateral cross-cousin marriage each in its own sphere, marriage with father's sister's daughter is not capable of attaining any other form than a multitude of little closed systems, juxtaposed to one another, without ever realizing a global structure."[12] He finds, moreover, that in his chosen ethnographic area of eastern Asia, the matrilateral form is more common than the patrilateral

[12]

one. And he goes on to take the stand that it is more common *because it is better* for society. Note his words well: "If then, in the last analysis, marriage with the daughter of the father's sister is less frequent than that with the daughter of the mother's brother, the reason is that the latter not only permits but favors a better integration of the group, while the former never succeeds in creating anything more than a precarious edifice, made of merely juxtaposed materials, obeying no plan of ensemble; and its texture is exposed to the same fragility as that of each of the little local structures of which it is composed."[13]

Are these words anything more than rhetoric? It is true that if, under the patrilateral rule, lineage B gives a woman to lineage A in one generation, it gets a woman back from the As in the next. Since under the matrilateral rule this cannot happen, one may reasonably argue that exchange in the latter rule is more roundabout, and if roundaboutness creates organic solidarity, and if organic solidarity is good for a society, then the matrilateral form is better than the patrilateral one. This is in fact Lévi-Strauss's argument. On the other hand, father's sister's daughter marriage, just like mother's brother's daughter marriage, requires at least three lineages; any one lineage is linked by marriage to two others in the ring, and the ring can be lengthened indefinitely. On all these counts it meets Lévi-Strauss's requirements for generalized exchange. The only difference is that the men of B lineage, defined either patrilineally or matrilineally, give women alternately to the As and to the Cs instead of always getting them from one and giving them to the other. We might even go on to argue that father's sister's daughter marriage makes for greater organic solidarity, as the specialization in marriage is determined by generation as well as by lineage, and so creates a more intricate intermeshing of groups. We raise this question but we do not insist on it, as our chief criticism of Lévi-Strauss is a far more searching one.

We also concede that there is at least one situation in which mother's brother's daughter marriage is clearly "better" than

[13]

father's sister's daughter. This is the situation described for the Kachin of upper Burma by Leach.[14] If the lineages of a society differ in social rank, and one of the aspects of the relationship between a superior lineage and a subordinate one is that the former gives women to the latter (or *vice-versa*), then mother's brother's daughter marriage is practicable as a formal structure and father's sister's daughter marriage is not. The latter would destroy the ranking by making any one lineage alternately superior and subordinate to aonther. But most societies practicing mother's brother's daughter marriage seem not to be stratified in the Kachin manner, and in any event "better" here means "more compatible with other aspects of the social structure" rather than "more creative of organic solidarity"—a very different matter.

A "final cause" theory

Our criticism of Lévi-Strauss goes deeper than anything we have said so far. But before we state our case, let us summarize Lévi-Strauss's, briefly but, we hope, fairly to him. Specialization of groups in their activities makes each dependent on the others. To get what it needs to maintain itself each must exchange with the others the products of the specialized activities. This is Durkheim's organic solidarity of groups within a society. Lévi-Strauss applies the idea to kin-groups and marriage. Women are the most highly valued of scarce goods, and so their exchange is most important in creating organic solidarity. The various rules of preferential marriage, from a simple incest taboo onwards, create exchanges of women between kin-groups, for if my group renounces marriage with its own women, it must get women from other groups. Indeed tribesmen adopt the different rules *in order to* create the exchanges and so the organic solidarity of their societies. Some rules, though, create a higher degree of organic solidarity than others. The more fully each kin-group is dependent, for getting its wives, on all the others, and thus the more "roundabout" the process of exchange, the greater the organic solidarity of the society. If one rule creates more organic solidarity than another, more tribes will adopt it. In the case we are using as a test, mother's brother's daughter marriage creates a higher degree of organic solidarity than father's sister's daughter marriage, and so more societies follow the former than the latter rule.

Like the rest of us, Lévi-Strauss is trying to answer the question: Why is a particular institution, or established norm of conduct, what it is? The answers given to this question have all, at one time or another, been called *functional* theories, but the word *function* has been used in several different senses, sometimes not distinguished from one another even within a single study. As we see it, the chief senses are three: 1. An institution is what it is because it results from the drives, or meets the immediate needs, of individuals or sub-groups within a society. Its function is to meet these needs. We may call this an individual self-interest theory, if we remember that interests may be other than economic. We may also call it Malinowskian functionalism and use Malinowski's theory of magic as an example.[15] 2. An institution is what it is because it meshes with other institutions in a society. This we may call quasi-mathematical functionalism: one institution is a function of others. An illustration might be the relation of matrilateral cross-cousin marriage to the ranking of lineages among the Kachin. 3. An institution is what it is because it is in some sense good for a society as a whole. The latter emphasis is what distinguishes this from an individual self-interest theory. The criterion of the good is often the maintenance of the society in stable equilibrium in the face of what are presumed to be disruptive tendencies: the function of an institution is the part it plays in maintaining societal equilibrium. This we may call Radcliffe-Brownian functionalism, and point to Radcliffe-Brown's theory of magic. But if Radcliffe-Brown asks no more of an institution than that it maintain any old equilibrium, Lévi-Strauss, whose theory falls into this class, goes much further. For him there are, so to speak, better and worse equilibria. An institution is what it is because it is good for a society in the sense of creating organic solidarity, and some institutions are, from this point of view, better than others.

One word about Radcliffe-Brown's functionalism. His position in fact combines theories of the second and third classes: "The *function* of any recurrent activity, such as the punishment of a crime, or a funeral ceremony, is the part it plays in the social life as a whole [class 2 theory], and therefore the contribution it makes to the maintenance of the structural continuity [class 3]."[16] What a lot is implied in that little word *therefore!* Now it is true that, if we know something less than everything about a society, and if, on the grounds of observations however rough, we may reasonably assume the society to be in equilibrium, then we may be able to make certain deductions, in areas not open to direct observation, about the nature of the society's institutions and their relations to one another. By the fact of equilibrium, the institutions and their relations become that much more nearly determinate. This is analogous to, if not as rigorous as, the use of a general equilibrium equation to make up a number of equations equal to the number of unknowns in solving a problem in mechanics. But a society does not *have* to be in equilibrium. Equilibrium is observed or assumed; it is not given automatically by the institutions of a society and their relations; and forces of the first and second classes, which in one balance may establish equilibrium, may in another produce a society changing rapidly, even catastrophically. There is certainly no reason to believe that an institution is what it is just because it helps establish stable equilibrium.

We have no doubt that theories of all three kinds say something true and important about social behavior. An institution like magic may meet individual needs, *and* mesh with other institutions, *and*—at times—contribute to the maintenance of stable equilibrium—all three. We are not forced to choose between Malinowski's and Radcliffe-Brown's approach. We need both. Our quarrel is in fact with scholars who try to explain social behavior with one of these theories alone. In his more *ex cathedra* pronouncements Radcliffe-Brown says the anthropologist may neglect the personal interest theories, on the grounds that the interests worked to create institutions at some time in the past, and the past is lost to students of societies—like most primitive ones—that have no history. To what extent this position is valid we shall perhaps consider later. Certainly Radcliffe-Brown as a fieldworker is an acute observer of personal interests. His practice is even better than his theory.

When a theory of the third class is used by itself to account for the existence of an institution we shall say that it is, for sociology, a *final-cause* theory. This comes close to being Lévi-Strauss's position: a rule of matrilateral cross-cousin marriage occurs more often than a patrilateral one because it creates a higher degree of organic solidarity for a *society*. We are not in the least concerned with the question whether organic solidarity is indeed good for a society, nor with the fact that Lévi-Strauss supplies no evidence, independent of the rules themselves, that societies with matrilateral rules are better integrated or indeed better off in any way than societies with patrilateral ones. All we are concerned with is the *nature* of Lévi-Strauss's theory. We argue that, to account for the adoption by a society of a particular institution, it is, in principle, never sufficient to show that the institution is in some sense good for the society, however that good may be defined. The weakness in all such theories was pointed out long ago by Aristotle. In his parable, "the house is there that men may live in it; but it is also there because the builders have laid one stone upon another."[17] Or, no final cause without an efficient cause. Lévi-Strauss's is not an evolutionary theory; it does not argue that the "worse" forms of marriage preceded the "better" in time of origin, but it bears some resemblance nevertheless to the Lamarckian theory of evolution, which held that "higher" animals have evolved from "lower" ones, without citing any mechanism by which this evolution might have taken place: teleology worked without help from nature. Science had no satisfactory theory of evolution until Darwin supplied efficient causes in random variation and the survival of the fittest, and even then an adequate theory of variation had to wait for the geneticists, if indeed we have a fully adequate one even now.

Any theory that will help us make sense of our data—that will redeem them from being *mere* data—is a useful one. If a final-cause theory will do so, we use it *faute de mieux*.[18] Lamarck's effort was not vain. But the very fact that a final-cause theory *will* order our data should prick us on all the more to find the efficient causes, for nature's efficient causes have a way of playing into the hands of her final ones. If we had no better way of making sense of the data than Lévi-Strauss's, we should have nothing to say against him. As it is, the very success of his effort has stimulated us into playing Darwin to his Lamarck.

Let us be quite clear: we have no doubt that some societies have evolved from good states to better ones. We are not among those that hold civilization no advance. We do believe it idle to say that societies adopted new forms of organization simply because these were better—for the societies—than the old. We must look for the specific conditions that enabled societies to adopt better forms, and this, we believe, requires our turning from functional theories of the third class to functional theories of the first and second.

In the course of trying to make the issue clear, we have not been altogether fair to Lévi-Strauss. We have implied that he has no efficient cause to account for the adoption by some societies of "better" marriage rules—matrilateral cross-cousin marriage rather than bilateral or patrilateral. He does not use, and in this we think him wise, a survival-value theory: we observe today a number of societies following the matrilateral rule because, by reason of having the rule, they were able to survive in competition with other societies. His is a much more powerful, if much more ancient, theory than this. Unlike some anthropologists of earlier generations, he has a high opinion of primitive men—or some of them—as thinkers, and he holds, if we understand him aright, that the members of some societies chose matrilateral cross-cousin marriage because they could "see," in much the same way that Lévi-Strauss himself can "see," that it was better than other forms.[19] He certainly cites many proverbs, current in societies following the matrilateral rule, that imply such recognition. We might argue that no society has trouble finding reasons why its institutions are better than those of others. These are rationalizations, or arguments after the fact. What we should like to have are arguments before the fact— those offered in favor of an institution *before* it was adopted. But since anthropologists have not observed societies in the process of adopting matrilateral cross-cousin marriage, we can hardly ask Lévi-Strauss to cite the debates.

In short, Lévi-Strauss's efficient cause is human intelligence, and this puts at stake nothing less than the nature of social development. We have no doubt that primitive men think rationally about their own societies. We do doubt that intelligent recognition that a certain institution would be good for a society is ever a sufficient—though it may be a necessary—condition for its adoption. If it were, the history of human society would be happier than we observe it to be. In personal behavior we have all grovelled with the honest poet who admitted *video meliora proboque, deteriora sequor*. If the problem is one of getting a *society* to adopt a better institution, when a large number of its members must take the risk of pursuing long-run, potential interests competing with short-run, actual ones—and this is precisely the problem with the adoption of matrilateral cross-cousin marriage, as Lévi-Strauss describes it—, we know bitterly how difficult the solution is. To account for success, we must bring to light the conditions under which some primitives are not only able to "see" a better institution but actually to attain it. We must also explain why, assuming the same average intelligence among primitive tribes, some are not. Even the Constitution of the United States would never have been adopted if it had not

[19]

served strong, short-run, personal, even selfish interests. In short we are again, as always, driven back to the arduous task of establishing the immediate determinants of different institutions. A theory of intelligence as the efficient cause, just as much as a pure final-cause theory, drives us back to explanations of the first and second classes.

An alternative theory: the patrilineal complex

If we find Lévi-Strauss's theory weak, the burden of proof is on us to supply one that will account for the facts more adequately. We have also committed ourselves to supplying a different *kind* of theory from his, one that will not appeal to what we have called a final cause, and that will (1) show the relation between different forms of unilateral cross-cousin marriage and other institutions, and (2) cite adequate individual motivation, aside from intellectual recognition that it is "good" for a society, to account for the adoption of a particular marriage rule. It is fair to say of Lévi-Strauss that he works with a very restricted model of society, a model that hardly includes more than the formal structure, as we have called it above, of lineages and the links between them created by different forms of preferential marriage.[20] For many purposes the use of a highly abstract model is illuminating. In this case, we believe the model is not lifelike enough to serve as a model at all. Using as our crucial test the two different forms of unilateral cross-cousin marriage, we shall try to relate them to aspects of kinship behavior other than those Lévi-Strauss usually takes into consideration.

Now the facts that Lévi-Strauss himself cites at once suggest an hypothesis different from his. Almost all the eastern Asian societies in which he finds mother's brother's daughter marriage preferred are organized in patrilineages. He does not lay any weight on this fact; he concerns himself with linearity, but not with the *kind* of linearity, and it is true that the differences in formal structure between the two forms of unilateral cross-cousin marriage persist whether the societies in question are patrilineal or matrilineal. But we, who are not bound to adopt Lévi-Strauss's model, at once ask ourselves: May not the type of unilateral cross-cousin marriage adopted by a society be associated with the type of linearity of its kin-groups?

What reasons have we for suspecting that such an association exists? We have learned from Radcliffe-Brown in his classic paper, "The Mother's Brother in South Africa,"[21] from Firth in his work on Tikopia,[22] and from Evans-Pritchard, Fortes, Gluckman, and the many other able British anthropologists who have worked in Africa, a good deal about the "patrilineal complex" in everyday kinship sentiment and activity. In a great many patrilineal societies in all parts of the world—just how many we cannot say, as this is a subject to which statistical studies have not yet addressed themselves—jural authority over ego is vested in his father and, more remotely, in his other patrilineal kinsmen of older generations. In these circumstances, a relationship builds up between ego and his father that may be marked on ego's part by admiration but also by respect and constraint, such as is often associated with the subordinate-superior relationship outside of kinship.

As it will play a big part in our argument, let us stop to make clear what we mean by *jural authority*. We shall say that a person has authority over others to the extent that they in fact carry out the wishes, suggestions, orders he addresses to them.[23] But in countless groups from factories to primitive tribes, persons who, by this definition, exercise authority do not exercise jural authority. The classic case is the woman who controls her family, though her husband is its acknowledged head. By *jural authority* we mean, then, legitimate or constituted authority, and a person holds jural authority over others when, according to the stated norms of his group, he has the right to give them orders and they have the duty to obey.[24] As norms must have some correspondence with actual behavior, so *de jure* authority must have some correspondence with *de facto*, and if persons of

[21]

a particular status in fact exercised chief authority over their groups, regularly and for a long time, we should expect their authority to become jural. Mothers have never been able to establish a legitimate matriarchy only because they have never bossed their families quite regularly enough.

A number of persons may hold jural authority over ego: in a patrilineal society his elder brother and his lineage head as well as his father. When we say that the locus of jural authority over ego in a patrilineal society is his father, we mean that the father is roughly equivalent to what a factory manager would call ego's first-line supervisor. We also imply a comparision. In this case we imply that his father has the recognized right to give orders to ego, and certain other persons do not—notably his mother's brother.

In the patrilineal complex, a relationship somewhat different from the father-son tie grows up between ego and his mother, who meets his compelling needs in infancy, and who is herself at least jurally subordinate to the father. She is a much more warm and nurturant figure. Apparently as a result of the identification of the mother with her brother, who is her protector, and the status of the latter as an older male without jural authority over ego, ego's behavior towards his mother's brother differs sharply from his behavior towards his father. The relationship varies somewhat from one patrilineal society to another. Ego may show great respect for mother's brother, but he also finds in him an intimate older friend, helper, and adviser. As Radcliffe-Brown pointed out, mother's brother in the patrilineal complex tends to become a kind of male mother, and in some societies is called by a word that means just this. The features that appear most often in the relationship seem to be four: 1. absence of jural authority, 2. the giving of help and advice by the mother's brother, as distinguished from orders, 3. frequent interaction, as when ego visits mother's brother from time to time, and 4. considerable freedom, as when either ego or mother's brother is free to use the other's possessions without asking permission.

Let there be no mistake, even about the obvious. In speaking of "the" mother's brother we do not assume that a mother has only one brother or even any brother at all. We mean mother's brother the status, not mother's brother the person, though no doubt when there are many brothers and many sisters, one of the brothers may well be closer than the others to a particular sister's son. Indeed some societies tend to pair off brothers and sisters, each member of such a couple being specially devoted to the other and the other's children.[25]

The data on father's sister in patrilineal societies are much less rich, but they suggest that she tends to become for ego a kind of female father, treated, as she is in Tikopia, with distance and respect.[26] For a fuller discussion of the propositions describing these interpersonal ties among kinsfolk, see G. C. Homans, *The Human Group*.[27] We admit the difficulty, which all novelists have encountered, of describing these ties in precise terms.

We suspect that mother's brother's daughter marriage may be particularly common in patrilineal societies because of the close nature of the tie between ego and mother's brother in these societies. We find in the structure of interpersonal relations the individual motivations, or efficient causes, for the adoption of a particular form of unilateral cross-cousin marriage. The motivations may take many and mixed forms, but they are all predicated on the nature of the ties. As he visits mother's brother often, ego will see a great deal of the daughter: contact will be established. As he is fond of mother's brother, and as mother's brother and his daughter in the patrilineal complex, the Oedipus Complex if you will, are themselves particularly close to one another, he will tend to get fond of the daughter. Their marriage will be sentimentally appropriate; it will cement the relationship. Or, if women are indeed scarce and valued goods, and ego is in doubt where he can get one, he will certainly be wise to ask his mother's brother, on whom he already has so strong a sentimental claim.

This latter motive is well documented for the patrilineal Hehe.

[23]

The Hehe allow other forms of marriage besides cross-cousin marriage, but one-quarter of all marriages are in fact with cross-cousins, real or classificatory, and of cross-cousin marriages four-fifths are with mother's brother's daughter and only one-fifth with father's sister's daughter. One native informant, translated freely, said: "Some people marry their cross-cousins because they realize that they are not of the group with whom marriage is forbidden. A child of an uncle (*i.e.* a nephew) says, 'I shall go and court my cousin, the child of my uncle, because we are related; they will give her to me, they will not refuse me, if my cousin loves me; my uncle will give her to me out of the kindness of his heart [literally "from a white liver"] because I am the child of his sister.'"[28] A similar kind of statement was made about father's sister's daughter marriage, but note that the characteristic patrilineal complex prevails among the Hehe, and the ethnologist says of father's sister: "She is treated with ceremonious respect, to an even greater degree than the uncle."[29]

In stating our argument, we have so far adopted the point of view of a male ego of the younger generation, but the same kinds of motivation might make this form of marriage particularly agreeable to the mother's brother too: he takes care of his beloved daughter by giving her to the man of the younger generation to whom he is sentimentally closest, even closer than he is to his own son. As for the girl, whose views we anthropologists hardly ever consider, whatever the primitives may do, she tends, in the patrilineal complex, to be closer to her father than is his son; through the identification of father and his sister, she would tend to find her elder confidante, outside of the family of orientation, in her father's sister, who is ego's mother. Mother's brother's daughter marriage (father's sister's son marriage from her point of view) is sentimentally appropriate for her too.

Our view that the efficient causes of matrilateral cross-cousin marriage are to be found in interpersonal relationships must now take us back to Lévi-Strauss. He recognizes that a tie between ego and mother's brother, of the kind we have described, exists in many of his patrilineal societies of eastern Asia. But since he tends to think of marriage rules as creating structures complete in themselves, which need not be considered in close relation to other aspects of kinship behavior, he does not lay any great weight on the fact. So far, indeed, as he does consider the role of the mother's brother, he seems to look on it as a consequence of marriage with mother's brother's daughter rather than as a possible cause.[30] But as it is not wholly clear that he takes this position, let us not attribute it to him but take it up in its own right as an obvious objection to our theory.

The position seems to us untenable for two reasons. First, the special relationship between ego and mother's brother seems to occur more often in patrilineal societies than mother's brother's daughter marriage, and the more general phenomenon can hardly be explained in terms of the less. Second, the position assumes that the mother's brother's role as father-in-law is the primary and governing factor. But the relationship between father-in-law and son-in-law is only less "difficult" than the mother-in-law relationships, and it is hard to see how it could give rise by itself to the characteristic "free and equal" relationship between ego and mother's brother. We argue instead that ego's tie with mother's brother *before* the latter becomes father-in-law is primary in influence as it is in time, and that one good reason why ego might want to marry his daughter is that the established relationship will soften the asperities of an otherwise "difficult" situation.

The reader may also object that we have put our argument in terms of the motives and behavior of individuals, whereas we promised earlier to follow Lévi-Strauss and deal with the various forms of cross-cousin marriage as norms stating the proper, not necessarily the actual behavior, for many individuals in a society. We hold, of course, that norms are not independent of actual behavior. When the social structures of many kin-groups in a society are similar, which is eminently the case with primitive societies, then many individuals will tend to develop similar sentiments and behavior towards similar kinsmen. For example, many egos will develop similar sentiments and behavior towards their respective mother's brothers. In time such sentiments and behavior will become recognized as the right and proper ones: they will be enshrined in norms. No doubt a norm, once established, has some measure of independent influence, if only because it is then taught to the young. Even then we do not believe that a norm can indefinitely maintain itself in the face of changes in social structure precipitating sentiments and behavior different from those originally enshrined in the norm. We deal with norms for convenience in argument, and because, as we shall see, most ethnographers tell us more about norms than about actual behavior. We admit that the relation between the two is elastic and not rigid, but we also hold that, in the long run and in a first approximation, behavior determines norms.

The matrilineal complex

Our theory is of little use unless it applies also to the other form of unilateral cross-cousin marriage—between ego and father's sister's daughter. If the patrilineal complex of relationships is associated with one marriage rule, the idea at once comes to mind that the matrilineal complex is associated with the other. Outside of Australia, Lévi-Strauss pays little attention to matrilineal societies, but of course the best-known of them is the society of the Trobriand Islands. In this society, as Malinowski described it, ego begins life in his father's house, but he belongs to his mother's lineage. His mother's brother holds jural authority over him; as he grows up he spends more and more time in his mother's brother's village, and when he marries his wife joins him there. In these circumstances, the relationship between ego and mother's brother much resembles that between ego and father in the patrilineal complex, and *vice-versa*, for ego and his father are close friends.[31]

Let there, again, be no ambiguity. We are speaking of mother's brother the status, not mother's brother the person. We have said that in the Trobriands mother's brother holds jural authority over ego. A more careful statement would be that, as he grows up, jural authority over ego is normally vested in the head of his sub-clan, who may well be one of his mother's brothers and who will, in any event, be one of his matrilineal, rather than patrilineal, kinsmen. We always, moreover, imply a comparison: the locus of jural authority is certainly mother's brother *rather* than father.

Moreover, just as there are at least two avunculates—patrilineal and matrilineal—so there are two amitates, and father's sister in the Trobriands plays a very different role from what she does in, for instance, a patrilineal society like Tikopia. Great freedom obtains between ego and herself; they may talk and joke about all matters, sexual or other; sexual intercourse between them is tolerated, and the preferred marriage is with the father's sister's daughter, not the mother's brother's.[32] This form of marriage is carried out in practice more often by members of the chiefly families than by commoners, but unlike some societies we shall mention later, the preference of the two classes is the same. Among the Hopi, another matrilineal society, the relationships between ego, father, mother's brother, and father's sister are described by Eggan in much the same terms as they are among the Trobriands by Malinowski: friendship and freedom to joke on sexual matters obtain between ego and father's sister, and there is some suggestion that in the past father's sister's daughter marriage was practiced.[33] In short, we suggest that the same kinds of motivation that make matrilateral cross-cousin marriage peculiarly appropriate in patrilineal society make patrilateral cross-cousin marriage peculiarly appropriate in matrilineal society. No doubt this motivation will not lead to effective results as often in matrilineal societies as in patrilineal ones. In the latter, ego in getting a wife depends on his ties with a man, his mother's brother; in the former on his ties with a woman, his father's sister, and a woman may well have less power of disposing of her daughter than a man has of his. So long as women are, in general and *de jure*, subordinated to men, matrilineal society can never be the mirror opposite of patrilineal. We believe, nevertheless, that the forces at work will be strong enough in some matrilineal societies to create a preference for father's sister's daughter marriage.

An hypothesis stated

When we first presented orally the substance of our present criticism of Lévi-Strauss,[34] we made, on the basis of the argument outlined above, the following prediction. Hypothesis: *Societies in which marriage is allowed or preferred with mother's brother's daughter but forbidden or disapproved with father's sister's daughter will be societies possessing patrilineal kingroups, and societies in which marriage is allowed or preferred with father's sister's daughter but forbidden or disapproved with mother's brother's daughter will be societies possessing matrilineal kin-groups.* Let methodological purists note that we made the prediction before we tried to verify it.

The hypothesis invites some explanatory comments. First, it is not an obvious and trivial one, in that it does not follow directly from the common taboo of ego's marriage within his lineage. In neither patrilineal nor matrilineal society is either cross-cousin a member of ego's lineage. Second, it says nothing about the determinants of unilateral cross-cousin marriage in general, as opposed to rules prescribing marriage with either or neither cross-cousin. *Given* unilateral cross-cousin marriage, it addresses itself to the question: What will determine the adoption of one form of unilateral cross-cousin marriage rather than the other? Third, it deals with the immediate cross-cousins and has nothing to say about more distant ones, such as mother's mother's brother's daughter's daughter.

Fourth, the hypothesis is a deduction from a theory rather than the theory itself. What we may call our general theory holds that the form of unilateral cross-cousin marriage will be determined by the system of interpersonal relations precipitated by a social structure, especially by the locus of jural authority over ego. Because we believe that this locus will be different in patrilineal society from what it is in matrilineal, we predict as a special hypothesis that one kind of unilateral cross-cousin marriage will be associated with patrilineal society, the other kind with matrilineal. For only one reason shall we begin by trying to verify our special hypothesis rather than our general theory: the ethnographic reports usually provide much better data on linearity than on systems of interpersonal relations. Note that we make our prediction in terms of the linearity of kin-groups, not in terms of the linearity of reckoning descent. In the absence of kin-groups that are in some measure corporate bodies, the mere reckoning of descent may mean little structurally. But when unilineal kin-groups are present, we may make a reasonable guess about the locus of jural authority over ego: it will at least lie within ego's own lineage. Even so, the connection between our general theory and our special hypothesis may well turn out to be loose. Our special hypothesis may turn out to be wrong, our general theory remaining right; or, conversely, our special hypothesis may turn out right for the wrong reasons— wrong in the sense of "other than those predicated in the general theory."

Finally, let us restate the differences between Lévi-Strauss's hypothesis and ours. He says that matrilateral cross-cousin marriage will occur in *more* societies than the patrilateral form because the former is *better* than the latter at creating organic solidarity. We say that, better or not, the matrilateral form will occur in patrilineal societies, the patrilateral form in matrilineal ones. Both of these hypotheses could conceivably be true, but it appears that in fact Lévi-Strauss rejects ours. He observes that the Mikir of Assam are organized in patrilineal, patrilocal clans and prefer mother's brother's daughter marriage, and that the nearby Garo are organized matrilineally and matrilocally but also prefer mother's brother's daughter marriage.[35] Both societies possess, in his terms, harmonic regimes. Hence, he says, "One can readily see that the structure of generalized exchange [matrilateral cross-cousin marriage] does not depend at all on linearity [*filiation*] but only on the harmonic character of the regime considered."[36] Because we anticipated this point, we were careful to explain above what Lévi-Strauss means by a harmonic regime. We neither accept nor reject Lévi-Strauss's claim that restricted exchange is associated with dysharmonic regimes. What we do reject is the claim that matrilateral cross-cousin marriage has nothing to do with linearity; we predict, Lévi-Strauss to the contrary, that it will tend to occur in patrilineal societies. If we are to show that our efficient-cause theory is more useful than his final-cause one, we are fortunate in having a problem in which the issue between them is clearly joined. We shall now see how far our hypothesis is verified.

Testing by the Murdock sample

In testing the hypothesis, we wanted to avoid, if we could, reviewing for ourselves the whole body of ethnographic literature. In these circumstances, the obvious man to ask for help was G. P. Murdock, and we submitted our hypothesis for testing against the data on the sample of 250 societies used in *Social Structure*.[37] Note that we tested on a world-wide basis and did not confine ourselves to Lévi-Strauss's chosen ethnographic area of Australia and eastern Asia. We are much indebted to Murdock for his help, but he must not be held responsible for any of our conclusions. He reported as follows:

1. Societies for which data are lacking on cross-cousin marriage or reported for only one cousin were omitted from the enumeration.
2. In 126 societies of the sample, marriage with either cross-cousin is forbidden or disapproved.
3. In 56 societies of the sample, marriage with either cross-cousin is allowed or preferred.

All of this information was useful in clearing the ground, but was not pertinent to our hypothesis. The next two findings *were* pertinent:

4. In 12 societies of the sample, marriage is allowed or pre-

ferred with mother's brother's daughter but forbidden or disapproved with father's sister's daughter. The societies are: Batak, Lakher, Lhota, Limba, Mbundu, Miwok, Murngin, Rengma, Sema, Thado, Timne, Venda. All of these societies, without exception, have patrilineal kin-groups, although the Murngin and Mbundu have full-fledged double descent (matrilineal as well as patrilineal kin-groups), and the Venda have survivalistic traces of matrilineal descent.

5. In 3 societies of the sample, marriage is allowed or preferred with father's sister's daughter but forbidden or disapproved with mother's brother's daughter. The societies are: Ila, Tismulun, Trobrianders. All three, without exception, have matrilineal kin-groups, the Ila having double descent.

These findings call for some immediate comments. First, if Murdock's sample is at all representative, either form of unilateral cross-cousin marriage must be a rare phenomenon, so that if frequency of occurrence is, as Lévi-Strauss seems to claim, a measure of the "goodness" of an institution, both forms must be fairly "bad." Second, Lévi-Strauss's statement that the matrilateral form is commoner than the patrilateral is confirmed, but the reason seems to be that more patrilineal societies practice unilateral cross-cousin marriage than matrilineal ones. And, third, whether or not one form produces a higher degree of organic solidarity than the other, the fact is that the different forms are associated with differences in the linearity of kingroups, and, so far as Murdock's sample is concerned, our hypothesis is confirmed.

Retesting with more societies

In fact it is confirmed all too well. Faced with the findings, one of the authors of this paper felt that they were too good to be true, and insisted on our looking for further examples of unilateral cross-cousin marriage, on the theory that there are no perfect correlations in the field of human behavior. But this

[31]

decision meant that we had to go to the ethnographic literature ourselves. We doubt that our search has been exhaustive. We got leads from Lévi-Strauss's book, from Murdock, and from others, and we followed them up to the point of diminishing returns, where the importance of this book did not, in our view, justify more work. But without question there are more societies practicing unilateral cross-cousin marriage than we have discovered.

The decision also meant that we had to face the same problems of taxonomy as did Murdock himself. If we are to test the hypothesis, each of its terms should refer to an unambiguously discriminable class of data, and this is not always the case. The word *society* itself is not easy to define. Is an Indian caste a society, and should castes be included in our list? Do the different Naga groups, Lhota, Rengma, and Sema, constitute separate societies? We raise these general questions without answering them, but our practice follows Murdock's. Nor is even the word *marriage* unambiguous. We decided that, even if we lacked other reasons for leaving the Nayar of Malabar off our list, we should reject them on the ground that nothing like marriage, in the sense of husband and wife "living together," exists among the Nayar, at least in that society's classical form.[38] And what do we mean by *unilineal kin-groups*—which raises the problem of double descent? The Mbundu, Murngin, and Venda may recognize matrilineal kin-groups, but what Leach calls the *local descent group*[39]—the core of kinsfolk associated generation by generation with a particular territory—consists in each of these societies of patrilineally-related men. We have had no trouble deciding that these societies are effectively patrilineal. The Ila, we confess, are not so easily handled, and we shall have to take up their case later.

Finally, how do we define *unilateral cross-cousin marriage?* We have chosen to consider only the immediate cross-cousins and not more distant ones. A more important question is whether we take the actual frequencies of the two different forms or what the natives say their preferences are—the official, expressed norms. It would be pleasant, because they would conform to our hypothesis, to include the matrilineal Yao, who formally approve marriage with either cross-cousin but actually marry father's sister's daughter more often than mother's brother's;[40] unpleasant to include the matrilineal Ashanti, who have the same formal rule but marry mother's brother's daughter more often.[41] Apart from our desire to meet Lévi-Strauss so far as possible on his own ground—and he deals regularly with marriage norms—, there are so few societies for which we have anything like marriage statistics that we have decided to classify according to formal preferences, as stated by the natives or the ethnographers. Under this rule, neither Yao nor Ashanti appear on our final list. In some societies, moreover, chiefs and other persons of rank follow marriage preferences decidedly different from those of commoners. Thus the heirs of chiefs among the matrilineal Haida often marry mother's brother's daughters for dynastic reasons, while the rule for the masses is father's sister's daughter.[42] When their formal preferences differ from those of commoners, we have decided to eliminate chiefs and the like from consideration, as introducing a complicating variable, that of rank, and we have accordingly moved the Haida from the list of bilateral societies to that of unilateral ones. We have also decided to give ourselves a little more leeway in deciding which societies are really unilateral. Murdock eliminated from his list all societies for which there was information on only one of the two female cross-cousins. Yet there is at least one society for which the ethnographic data show a decided unilateral preference without specifically ruling out the cross-cousin on the other side. We are ready to presume that this society is unilateral and have accordingly included the Garo on our final list. In this we follow Lévi-Strauss, but we differ from him in excluding the Khasi. They allow marriage with either cross-cousin *after the death of mother's brother or father* respectively, but they tend to disapprove of father's sister's daughter's marriage even then.[43]

[33]

In our view, their case is ambiguous because they allow unilateral cross-cousin marriage part of the time and forbid it part of the time. Obviously we do not have space to justify our decision in the case of every society, but we are ready to defend ourselves if attacked.

Our final list—final only so long as further relevant societies are not dug out of the literature—is as follows:[44]

1. *Patrilineages—matrilateral form preferred:*
   Altaians and Teleuts, Batak, Gilyak, Gold, Kachin, Karadjeri, Lakher, Lhota, Limba, Lovedu, Mbundu, Mende, Miwok, Murngin, Rengma, Sandawe, Sema, Thado, Timne, Venda, Wik-Munkan (Archer River group), Yir-Yoront.
2. *Patrilineages—patrilateral form preferred:*
   Kandyu, Sherente.
3. *Matrilineages—matrilateral form preferred:*
   Garo, Kaonde, Kaska, Siriono.
4. *Matrilineages—patrilateral form preferred:*
   Haida, Ila, Tismulun, Tlingit, Trobrianders.

If we put the results in a four-fold table, we get the following:

TABLE 1

	Kin-Groups	
Preferred marriage	Patrilineal	Matrilineal
Mother's brother's daughter	22	4
Father's sister's daughter	2	5

The general characteristics of this distribution are similar to those of the distribution obtained from the Murdock sample. Unilateral cross-cousin marriage of either kind is still a rare phenomenon. The matrilateral form still is more frequent of occurrence than the patrilateral one, but this still seems to depend, not on the inherent "goodness" of the form, but on the fact that there are more patrilineal societies on our list than matrilineal ones and they tend to prefer the matrilateral form. For, although our perfect correlation has gone, and the six societies in classes 2 and 3 above now constitute exceptions to our hypothesis, the relationship is still in the direction predicted by the hypothesis, and it is still statistically significant. (P=0.009 by Fisher's Exact Test.)[45] Contrary to Lévi-Strauss, linearity *is* a determinant of the form of unilateral cross-cousin marriage. A further question is whether the proportion of patrilineal societies in our list is larger than the proportion in the world at large; that is, whether *even* more patrilineal societies practice unilateral cross-cousin marriage than the number of *all* patrilineal societies, as compared with the number of *all* matrilineal societies, would lead us to expect. Now the matrilineal/ patrilineal ratio in Murdock's total sample is 0.45 and in our list 0.375. We got absolutely more patrilineal societies than we had a right to expect. We do not know that we can properly show the difference to be significant, but if it *were* significant it would still suggest that linearity makes a difference to unilateral cross-cousin marriage, in that more patrilineal societies practice either of its forms than do matrilineal ones. Or, in Lévi-Strauss's terms, if the matrilateral form is "good," it is particularly good for patrilineal societies.

Testing the general theory

The next question is: Do we need to feel discouraged because our predicted correlation did not turn out on retest to be more significant? Can we recapture a really high correlation? There may be a way. The reader will remember that the hypothesis we have just tested was a special deduction from a more general theory, according to which differences in marriage preferences were related to differences in systems of interpersonal relations among kinsfolk. If, in particular, the relation between ego male and mother's brother was "close" and that with father's sister "distant," we expected unilateral cross-cousin marriage, provided it existed at all, to take place with mother's brother's daughter. If the roles were reversed, we expected marriage with father's sister's daughter. Of course these words "close" and "distant" are only shorthand descriptions of the facts.

We further held that the system would take the first form when father held jural authority over ego, the second when mother's brother held it; that, in short, the locus of jural authority is an important determinant of systems of interpersonal relationships, and these of marriage preferences. Because we further believed that father would be apt to hold jural authority over ego in a society of patrilineal kin-groups, and mother's brother in a society of matrilineal kin-groups, we predicted that mother's brother's daughter marriage would be preferred in the former, father's sister's daughter in the latter. We decided to test our general theory in the form of this special hypothesis, for the reason that ethnographic reports usually contain more adequate information on linearity than on interpersonal relations.

But *some* reports do tell us a little about interpersonal ties, and so the following questions come up: In the societies conforming to our special hypothesis, what evidence is there for the kinds of interpersonal relations we should anticipate from the general theory? Or, were we right for the right reasons? And in the societies that are exceptions to our hypothesis, what evidence is there for the kind of interpersonal relations we should anticipate from the general theory, even though linearity is not as predicted? In particular, is the assumption on which we derived the hypothesis—that the locus of jural authority over ego is the father in all patrilineal societies, the mother's brother in all matrilineal ones—justified in fact? Or, were we wrong for the right reasons? Is, in short, our general theory more adequate than our special hypothesis? To answer this question, we shall have to examine whatever evidence on interpersonal relations exists for societies on our list, particularly evidence on the locus of jural authority over ego and on ego's ties with father, father's sister, and mother's brother.

Patrilineal-matrilateral societies (Class 1)

We shall take first the societies that conform to our special hypothesis. For none of the patrilineal-matrilateral societies, except the Murngin and Yir-Yoront, whom we shall consider later, is there reason to suspect that the locus of immediate jural authority over ego lies in any person but his father. For thirteen of these societies—Batak, Gilyak, Karadjeri, Lakher, Lhota, Lovedu, Mbundu, Mende, Murngin, Sema, Venda, and Wik-Munkan— the reported data suggest, in our view, a relationship between ego and mother's brother that has at least some points in common with the relationship in the classic patrilineal complex as it exists, for instance, in Tikopia, and which is the relationship our general theory expected to find associated with mother's brother's daughter marriage. The evidence is perhaps least clear for the Mbundu. In this society, where the local descent groups are patrilineal but dispersed matrilineages are also present, the mother's brother held more jural authority over ego in the past than he does today.[46] As for father's sister, we have information on her from only the Lovedu, Mbundu, Murngin, and Venda, but in every one of these cases she appears in the role we expected from our general theory—a "female father" in a situation where the father is a figure of authority and respect. As for the other societies, we have been unable to consult the Russian sources personally, and the rest do not provide adequate information on interpersonal relationships.

By way of illustration, let us look briefly at interpersonal ties among the Lovedu.[47] Of the father we learn this: "Because he spends most of his time with the men, there is little personal contact between father and young children. . . . The boy finds that his father admonishes him or shows displeasure when he cries and on occasion inculcates manly virtues. The father keeps his distance, yet he becomes the personification of manly ideals, and a boy tries to be like his father. The father has authority, but his authority is never oppressive like that of European fathers, whose children live in much closer contact with them.

If a boy has done wrong or let the cattle stray, he will avoid his father by not making an appearance at home till after dark." Of the father's sister: "Derived from the brother-sister relationship is that of the father's sister, who is accorded honor and respect by the children of the house she has established." Her role in the patrilineage is that of a priestess.

As for the matrilineal kinsfolk, "the greatest of all bonds between a man and his mother's side of the family is conceived by the Lovedu to be one of love. There is a saying, usually quoted by women, . . . which, freely translated, means, 'Love lies on the mother's side of the family; ownership on the father's.' " "Ownership," we suspect, refers here to all those jural rights of control that are crucial in determining the respect relationship. Among mother's kin, ego among the Lovedu is particularly close to mother's mother, and his relationship with mother's brother, while friendly, is tinged with respect: "Your mother's brother may be kind to you, but you have to show him respect: if he asks you to go on a message or to help him in the fields, you cannot refuse; while, if he needs you, you may be sent to herd for him or help nurse his small children." Finally, "the sister's son is a potential son-in-law, who is accorded great honor in the household of his mother's brother." We could indeed state our general theory loosely as: Where a man finds love in one generation, he will find it in the next.

We must now meet an obvious issue head-on. Earlier, we quoted a Hehe informant who said that ego sought mother's brother's daughter in marriage *because* of his close sentimental ties with mother's brother. For none of the present societies do the sources provide explicit statements of this sort. We nevertheless believe that the sentimental tie is a necessary, if not a sufficient, cause of the marriage preference, in the special sense of preceding it in time. We are in no position to demonstrate this, and even if we were, we should expect the "cause" to drop out of explicit recognition by the natives. Without doubt the marriage preference has existed in these societies for some length of time, in the course of which it has become an established norm and linked with aspects of social organization other than the sentimental tie. Among the Lovedu, for instance, it is linked with the transmission of bridewealth. The natives may even come to feel that the system it creates is "good" in the same sense that Lévi-Strauss does. To the norm, to the other linkages, to the advantages, rather than to the sentimental tie, the natives may well refer if asked to account for the marriage preference. From the fact that the nature of the linkages with other institutions varies more from society to society than the sentimental tie itself, we might argue that the latter was the more important, because more nearly universal, determinant: marriage with mother's brother's daughter is found in the presence of the sentimental tie with mother's brother far more often than in that of the transmission of bridewealth. But all we insist on is the sheer association between different forms of unilateral cross-cousin marriage and different systems of interpersonal relations, including different *loci* of jural authority over ego. From either variable we can predict the other. We believe present association betrays ultimate origin; the history of some institutions is repeated every generation; to some unknown degree the energies that maintain a system are the ones that created it, and to this degree Radcliffe-Brown is wrong in holding that the history of primitive institutions is forever lost to us. We believe this; we do not know that we can prove it, and in any event it becomes irrelevant in the face of the present association of institutions.

The problem of analysing systems of interpersonal relations is further complicated by the tendency of every kinship system to build its own backfires. Thus if mother's brother has many sister's sons, real or classificatory, competing for his daughter, and he has the power to withhold her from any one of them, this fact might tend to create tension between ego and mother's brother and spoil what might otherwise have been a beautiful friendship. A sentimental tie may create an institution and, in so doing, help poison itself. This may explain why, among the

Murngin, ego may be close to mother's brother but is even closer to mother's mother's brother.[48] Indeed we should expect the tie between ego and mother's brother to be most fully friendly in a patrilineal society like Tikopia that does *not* practice mother's brother's daughter marriage.

If, again, the sentimental tie with his mother's brother is very important to ego, he may hesitate to offend mother's brother, which may give the latter *de facto* authority over ego, however little he may have *de jure*. Thus we learn of the Mende, one of the societies of the present class, "In terms of family law, to disobey one's uncle is an even graver offence than disobedience of one's father and may provoke a more serious curse."[49] On this point we are fully in agreement with Radcliffe-Brown's discussion of the mother's brother's curse: "This is sometimes interpreted as though it means that the mother's brother regularly exercises authority over his nephew, and that his authority is greater than that even of a father. I suggest that the proper interpretation is that the mother's brother will be the last person to use his power of cursing, and that it is for this reason that it is feared more than the curse of the father."[50] In accepting this view, we must still admit that these "backfires" add to the ambiguity of interpersonal relations.

We turn last to the difficult case of the Yir-Yoront of the Cape York peninsula, Australia. They are organized in patrilineages, approve marriage with mother's brother's daughter, but forbid it with father's sister's daughter, and thus conform to our special hypothesis.[51] But it is at least doubtful that they also conform to our general theory. Both father and father's sister spoil ego until he is well into manhood—not usual roles for either in the patrilineal complex.[52] Ego's mother is his chief disciplinarian, at least before his adolescence, and shares this role to some extent with mother's brother, to whom ego pays the greatest respect.[53] It is perhaps significant that marriage is uxorilocal, at least for its first years. Our information on this group is inadequate, but if ego's relation to father and father's sister is as described, and

[40]

if mother's brother is indeed the chief male authority over ego, we should, according to our general theory, have expected to find marriage with father's sister's, not mother's brother's, daughter. In this one society we were right for the wrong reasons.

In a letter to the authors Professor Radcliffe-Brown makes a comment that may throw light on interpersonal relations among the Yir-Yoront. In many Australian tribes, he says, "the discipline of very young children is left to the mother and the other women of the horde. A father does not punish and may even not scold his infant children, but if they misbehave he will scold the mother and perhaps give her a blow with a stick. He regards the mother as responsible for misbehavior by very young children. When they are a little older, the father undertakes the education of the boys but leaves the education of the girls to the mother and the women of the horde. But the father behaves affectionately and is very little of a disciplinarian. Discipline for a boy begins when he approaches puberty and is exercised by the men of the horde. The big change comes with the initiation ceremonies when, in some tribes, the father, by a ceremonial (symbolic) action, hands over his son to the men who will carry out the initiation rites. During the initiation period of several years the boy is subjected to rigid and frequently painful discipline by the men other than his father."

This may explain why, among the patrilineal Yir-Yoront, the father is not ego's chief disciplinarian, and the relationship can be an affectionate one. We might therefore expect father's sister's daughter marriage to be sentimentally possible, but among the Yir-Yoront mother's brother's daughter marriage in fact occurs. Why? We might argue as follows. Though chief authority over ego is not exercised by the father, it *is* exercised by the other men of the horde, and in a patrilineal society these are at least men "on the father's side of the family" such as father's brothers—they are ego's patrikin. The patrilineage, if not the father himself, represents authority, and this might still be enough to throw marriage to the mother's side. We raise this as a question. We certainly do not insist on it as an argument, and we shall continue to treat the Yir-Yoront as an exception to our general theory.

Something of the same sort, though apparently in lesser degree, seems to be true of another Australian tribe, the Murngin. Authority over ego is vested in his patrilineage, but ego's own father does not correct him and acts only as a kind of older brother. Since the other interpersonal relations are of the kind we expect in the patrilineal complex, we do not consider the Murngin a full exception to our general theory, as we do so consider the Yir-Yoront.

To sum up the evidence on patrilineal-matrilateral societies: in those societies for which we have any evidence on interpersonal relations and the locus of jural authority over ego, the evidence is that, with the exception of the Yir-Yoront, the societies conform both to our special hypothesis and to our general theory. To this extent, we were right for the right reasons.

Matrilineal-patrilateral societies (Class 4)

The other class of societies that conforms to our special hypothesis is the matrilineal-patrilateral one. If our general theory is correct, we should expect to find that jural authority over ego in these societies is vested in his mother's brother, and that he is less "close" to mother's brother, closer to father and father's sister, than he is in the patrilineal complex. This is true, as Malinowski showed, of the Trobrianders, and we have cited the evidence above. Among the Haida, we know that ego, after about the age of ten, goes to live permanently with his mother's brother, who thereafter is in charge of his discipline. Our source tells us little of ego's sentimental ties with mother's brother and father, but father's sister, unlike her counterpart among, for instance, the patrilineal Venda, is a friendly and nurturant figure. Among other things, she nurses ego when he is sick.[54]

As for the Tlingit, neighbors of the Haida on the Northwest

Coast, the "ideal" marriage is clearly with father's sister's daughter, though a young man of rank, as among the Haida, may marry mother's brother's daughter. Mother's brother holds jural authority over ego, and the following passage implies a difference, of the expected kind, between ego's attitude to father and to mother's brother: "The father-child tie is one which is stressed on all possible occasions. . . . To address or to refer to a group as 'Kagwantan children' brings pleased smiles to their faces. Perhaps it recalls, at least to the men, a carefree childhood in their father's house before they had to submit to the discipline of their uncle in order to prove their manhood and enter upon their matrilineal inheritance."[55]

For the Tismulun, we have no information on interpersonal relations, but one structural fact is especially worth citing. Marriage is permitted and approved between ego and father's sister's daughter *or* mother's brother's daughter's daughter.[56] Since the latter is not by our definition cross-cousin marriage, it does not fall within the scope of our hypothesis. But if the reader will refer to Figure 2 above, he will note that, in the structure created in a matrilineal society by patrilateral cross-cousin marriage regularly followed, ego's mother's brother's daughter's daughter stands in the relation of father's sister's daughter, *i.e.*, preferred spouse, to ego's own sister's son, *i.e.*, his matrilineal heir.

It might be argued that the Ila do not fall within the scope of our hypothesis because they are not even "effectively matrilineal" in the sense that the Mbundu are effectively patrilineal. According to Smith and Dale,[57] they are organized in exogamous matriclans, and there is some evidence that succession to positions of authority is matrilineal. But the members of a clan are physically dispersed: the core of the lineage does not consist, as it seems to consist in other societies of this class, of a group of matrilineally-related men living in the same place. Instead, the usual residence group consists of "a man, his wives, his married sons, and the latters' children, his unmarried children, and his servants and slaves."[58] Such a local descent group, which is called *lunungu,* might well be considered a patrilineage.

But even if, on these grounds, the Ila should be thrown out of court as far as our special hypothesis is concerned, they fit our general theory well. Smith and Dale are clear that marriage is allowed with father's sister's daughter and not with mother's brother's, and that mother's brother has greater power over ego than father has: "The mother's brother is a person of vast importance, having the power even of life and death over his nephews and nieces, which no other relations, not even the parents have; he is to be held in honor even above the father. This is *avunculi potestas,* which among the Ba-Ila is greater than *patria potestas.*"[59]

For the matrilineal-patrilateral societies, the evidence on interpersonal relations and the locus of jural authority is, except for the Trobrianders, scanty, but what there is is all in accordance with our general theory. Once more we were right for the right reasons.

Matrilineal-matrilateral societies (Class 3)

Let us now turn to the societies (classes 2 and 3 above) that stand as exceptions to our special hypothesis. If we are honest, we must confess that we are anxious to get rid of them if we may do so with honor—which in this case means showing, that, though they do not conform to our special hypothesis, they do nevertheless conform to our general theory. We shall take first the matrilineal-matrilateral societies.

Although what is at this writing our only printed source on the matrilineal Kaonde—Melland's *In Witch-Bound Africa*—is thoroughly unsatisfactory, it does state clearly that marriage with mother's brother's daughter is "permitted" but with father's sister's daughter prohibited.[60] A letter from Victor Turner of the Rhodes-Livingstone Institute, reporting recent field work among the Kaonde, suggests that their rule is in fact bilateral, but for the sake of consistency we shall abide by our printed sources and not throw the Kaonde out of court. Melland says almost nothing about interpersonal relations, except that ego male tends strongly to avoid father's sister and mother-in-law. In short, the Kaonde stand as an exception to our special hypothesis, but we have no evidence whether or not they conform to our general theory—save only for the ego-father's sister tie, which is of the sort expected by our general theory and is very different from the corresponding tie in societies like the Trobrianders and the Haida of the matrilineal-patrilateral class. In another respect too the Kaonde differ from the Trobrianders: with the former marriage is uxorilocal, with the latter virilocal.[61] We shall have to deal with residence more thoroughly than we have done so far, and find in it our first hint of the reason why our special hypothesis admitted so many exceptions.

With the Kaska of the Canadian Northwest, we are in a better position. They are organized in two matrilineal "sides" or moieties, the members of neither of which are concentrated in one area, and "the importance of the moiety is slight."[62] Marriage is forbidden with father's sister's daughter, preferred with mother's brother's daughter. As with the Kaonde, marriage is uxorilocal: a man settles down in a log house of his own in the neighborhood of his father-in-law, the household consisting of the married couple, their children, perhaps aged grandparents and orphaned children of kin. And now we come to what, in our eyes, is a crucial point: "Authority in the family is ideally vested in the husband. . . . The authority of the husband is maintained even if the family happens to contain a grandparent. Although under conditions of matrilocal residence, a father may offer advice to his son-in-law, such advice is not given in an authoritative fashion and, once the marriage is established, does not dispute the authority of the husband. The importance of the father is often reflected in the fact that, despite the system of matrilineal moieties, family names follow the patrilineal line."[63] We are given, moreover, just enough information on mother's brother to suggest that ego's relationship with him resembles what it is in the patrilineal complex, where jural authority is likewise vested in the father: "A woman's brother refers to his sister's daughter as his own child. . . . A reciprocal term is employed between a boy and his mother's brother. It was said to be all right to 'talk fun,' *i.e.* refer to salacious matters, with mother's brother. The relationship of a child to its father's sister could not be observed."[64]

The next member of this class is the Siriono, nomad hunters and gatherers of eastern Bolivia. They possess matrilineal extended families. Marriage is forbidden with father's sister's daughter, preferred with mother's brother's daughter.[65] Again, as with the Kaonde and Kaska, marriage is uxorilocal, but when the son-in-law, upon marriage, moves next to his parents-in-law, he may not have to move *far*, as he is apt to be living already in the same house. "An extended family is made up of all females in a direct line of descent, plus their spouses and their unmarried children." And now we come again to the crucial point: "Within the nuclear family, authority is patripotestal. . . . The extended family is generally dominated by the oldest active male. Although his power is not supreme like that of the father in a nuclear family, younger members of the extended family pay heed to his words." We learn nothing of sentimental ties between kinsmen, save for a little more about parents and children: "Between parents and young children there is little reserve. As children grow older, however, they are expected to respect and obey their parents, who treat them roughly in case they do not."[66] This differs greatly from the father-son tie in the Trobriand-type matrilineal complex. Note that under the given conditions—extended families whose persistent core consists of matrilineally-related women, plus uxorilocal marriage with mother's brother's daughter—ego is *never*, as he in the Trobriands, under the jural authority of his mother's brother *before marriage*, but under that of his father. *After marriage* he may come under some slight control by his mother's brother, provided the latter is the oldest active male of the extended family into which ego has married and moved.

We have stretched a point in including the Garos of Assam in our list, because our sources do not indicate that marriage with father's sister's daughter is forbidden or disapproved.[67] But mother's brother's daughter marriage is clearly a preferred form, and in some other respects the Garo resemble the Kaska and the Siriono. They are organized in matrilineal exogamous clans;[68] jural authority over ego before marriage is certainly vested in the father in the case the latter is a village headman,[69] and we suspect also when he is only head of a household. Uxorilocal marriage is again the rule, and authority in local groups seems to pass from father-in-law to son-in-law, who, if he marries mother's brother's daughter, will also be the former's sister's son, that is, one of his matrilineal heirs.

In short, the matrilineal-matrilateral societies are clear exceptions to our special hypothesis, but whenever we have information they turn out to conform to our general theory. That is, the locus of jural authority (in the father) and the system of interpersonal relations among kinsfolk are what we should expect, according to our general theory, to find associated with mother's brother's daughter marriage. We were wrong for the right reasons.

It should now also be clear why our special hypothesis admitted these exceptions. We derived it from our general theory on the assumption that in matrilineal societies jural authority over ego would always be vested in mother's brother, and this is not the case. That is, we assumed, when we ought to have known better, that there was only one main matrilineal complex —the Trobriand type—, whereas in fact there are at least two. In the Trobriand-Haida complex ego typically goes to live with his mother's brother before marriage and brings his wife to stay with him there: marriage is virilocal. From an early age jural authority over ego is vested in mother's brother, and interpersonal relations are very different from what they are in the patrilineal complex. In the Kaska-Garo complex, ego continues to live with his father until he marries, when he goes to stay at his wife's place: marriage is uxorilocal. At least until ego marries, jural authority over him is vested in his father, and this is made all the more possible by the fact that the adult males of the mother's—and ego's—matrilineage have moved out. Interpersonal relations much resemble those of the patrilineal complex. The two matrilineal complexes are quite different from one another. We shall return to these differences later.

Patrilineal-patrilateral societies (Class 2)

The last and smallest class of exceptions is the patrilineal-patrilateral one. Our printed source on the Kandyu of the Cape York peninsula, Australia, shows them to prefer father's sister's daughter marriage and forbid mother's brother's daughter. In a letter to one of the authors, A. R. Radcliffe-Brown, an authority of especially great weight in the field of Australian kinship, expresses doubt that the Kandyu rule is really patrilateral: a man may marry the daughter of his own father's younger, but not older, sister, and the daughter of a classificatory, but not true, mother's brother. We should probably drop the Kandyu, like the Kaonde, from our list, much to the improvement of our correlation coefficient, since both stand as exceptions to our special hypothesis, but by our principle of respecting the printed sources we shall leave them in.

The only information we are given on interpersonal relations among the Kandyu is not very helpful: "The more extensive hunting grounds of the forest country, and consequent wandering habits of the Kandyu involve a loosening of the close tie with the mother's clan grounds, and a strengthening of the solidarity of the father's clan, a woman being glad to identify herself with her hereditary ground and clan by giving her daughter to her brother's son."[70] This tells us nothing about the locus of jural authority and almost nothing about interpersonal relations. The Kandyu must remain, like the Kaonde, an unexplained exception to our special hypothesis.

The only other member of this class is an exceptionally interesting one, the Sherente of Brazil, for whom we have much better, though still inadequate, information. The Sherente are organized in patrilineal exogamous moieties, each of which is further divided into three patrilineal exogamous clans, and there is one further clan, fitted only loosely into the moiety organization.[71] The clans are without significance in economic activity, warfare, or religious ceremonial. Households contain nuclear families: parents and children. The effective working groups in hunting, shifting agriculture, and ceremonial are the associations, of which there are four. Each of the four has two leaders, one from each moiety, and each of the leaders directs, in the work of the association, the members that belong to the moiety *other than his own.*[72] About the age of eight, when he becomes of some use at work, a boy joins one of the associations, and generally he is *"kept from joining his father's organization."*[73] At the same time, he leaves his father's house for a special association hut for bachelors.[74]

Note that although this society is formally patrilineal, jural authority over ego male is not, after an early age, vested in his father, but in one of the leaders of his association. Even if his father belongs to the same association, which is not generally the case, ego is not bossed by him but by an older member of the other moiety, who must therefore belong to ego's mother's moiety. His boss might be his mother's brother, though he might also be his father's sister's husband. In short, this may be a patrilineal society, but it is not a patripotestal one.

Marriage is, after the first year, patrilocal. It is permitted with father's sister's daughter but not with mother's brother's daughter. This is perfectly compatible with the existence of two exogamous patrilineal moieties and six exogamous patrilineal clans. But our source also says: "There seems to be a tendency to marry close matrilineal kin so long as the prohibited degrees are avoided," and cites an example of marriage with mother's brother's daughter's daughter, who was a member of the loosely-linked seventh clan.[75] We have noted above the structural connection between father's sister's daughter marriage and mother's brother's daughter's daughter marriage.

Of interpersonal ties we learn little, and that little has to do with girls, whereas most ethnographic reports tell us chiefly about the ties of men. Girls belong to women's associations, which have no economic significance, and girls do not leave home to live in a special hut. Up to the age of six, "there is little punishment; but a change occurs as soon as the mother begins to employ her daughter in the household, where she is made especially to tend younger siblings and the kitchen. Then the women frequently bawl at their daughters and beat them in a manner that would horrify any Timbira mother. I have also seen a father strike his daughter because she disobeyed her mother. Incidentally, similar treatment is meted out to boys of this age. . . . I was told that paternal and maternal uncles were equally esteemed, but concrete example suggest that only a girl's maternal uncle plays a significant part. . . . He distributes food among the members of the name-conferring society when his niece gets her name, and in return obtains decorations for her. He leads his niece to her bridegroom and dissolves an un-tenable marriage by bringing her back from her husband's to her father's house. He allows a virgin the formal choice between wedlock and the wanton's state, and in case of premarital de-floration calls the culprit to account."[76] Note that, with father's sister's daughter marriage, this bridegroom to whom mother's brother leads his sister's daughter is the mother's brother's own son. And does this account suggest that mother's brother has jural authority over a girl, as he might well have over a boy, if they belonged to the same association and mother's brother was one of its leaders?

Both the Kandyu and the Sherente are exceptions to our spe-cial hypothesis. For the Kandyu we do not have the information to say whether or not they conform to our general theory. The Sherente conform in a negative sense: authority over ego *is not*, after an early age, vested in his father, which is what we should expect from the theory. We cannot say that it *is* positively vested in his mother's brother, but only that, as a member of one of the actual working groups of this society, ego is at least bossed by a member of his mother's moiety.

To sum up our findings on all four classes: among those societies on our list for which we have some information on interpersonal relations and the locus of jural authority, there is only *one* that stands as a true exception to our general theory—the Yir-Yoront of the patrilineal-matrilateral class. Specifically, the following is a highly significant proposition: *Societies in which marriage is allowed or preferred with mother's brother's daughter but forbidden or disapproved with father's sister's daughter will be societies in which jural authority over ego male, before marriage, is vested in his father or father's lineage, and societies in which marriage is allowed or preferred with father's sister's daughter but forbidden or disapproved with mother's brother's daughter will be societies in which jural authority over ego male, before marriage, is vested in his mother's brother or mother's brother's lineage.*

A classification of local descent groups

In determining whether the societies on our list conformed to our general theory, we have learned more about their social organization than just their linearity and marriage rules. Some of these facts fit so well into a classification made by Murdock[77] of types of *clans* and by Leach[78] of what he calls *local descent groups,* that we are encouraged to discuss the classification briefly. In most primitive societies we observe kin-groups each of which occupies a particular territory generation after generation. How is the continuity of such groups maintained? In particular, what rules of descent and residence determine what category of persons shall form the continuing core of such groups? We also observe that certain persons exercise authority over others in these groups. What rules determine succession to authority?

Two rules that seem, in practice, to be often obeyed are the following:

[51]

1. The continuing core of the local group consists of persons of the same sex and the same lineage.

2. Authority is transmitted from men to men of the same local group and lineage.

Murdock and Leach, each in his own way, suggest that the main possibilities of constituting local descent groups according to these rules are three:

A. *Patrilineages with patrilocal (virilocal) residence at marriage.* Under these circumstances, the continuing core of the local group consists, generation by generation, of *patrilineally-related men* (fathers and sons). The women of the lineage move out, the women of other lineages move in, at marriage. Authority is transmitted from father to son, and there is no problem in following the rule of transmission, as both men, throughout life, are members of the same local group. For men, this is a zero-move type of society. This class seems to include most of our patrilineal-matrilateral societies (Class 1 above). We shall want to ask ourselves why this solution is adopted far more frequently than the others.

B. *Matrilineages with avunculocal (virilocal) residence at marriage.* Here the continuing core of the local group consists of *matrilineally-related men* (mother's brothers and sister's sons). The daughters of the men move out, the women of other lineages move in, at marriage. Authority is transmitted from mother's brother to sister's son, but there is a problem in following the rule of transmission, which is solved by the sister's son moving from his father's to his mother's brother's local group before marriage. For men, this is a one-move (before marriage) type of society. This class seems to include most of our matrilineal-patrilateral societies (Class 4 above), with the exception of the Ila.

The Trobrianders meet the requirements of this class under all conditions except one, but that one is particularly interesting to us. If ego marries father's sister's daughter, he may be allowed to remain in his father's village, which is also the village associated with his father's matrilineage, including father's sister and her daughter. Then only does the "closeness" of father and son, in a society in which jural authority over ego is vested in mother's brother, overcome the rule of avunculocal residence.

C. *Matrilineages with matrilocal (uxorilocal) residence at marriage.* Here the continuing core of the local group consists of *matrilineally-related women* (mothers and daughters). The men of the lineage move out, the men of other lineages move in, at marriage. Authority is transmitted from father-in-law to son-in-law, and there is an obvious problem in following the rule of transmission. It can be solved by mother's brother's daughter marriage, in which case father-in-law and son-in-law are also mother's brother and sister's son. That is, they are men who, when the transmission of authority takes place, sometime between the marriage of the latter and the death of the former, are members of the same local group and the same lineage, though the lineage is different from that of the women who form the constituting core of the local group. For men, this is a one-move (at marriage) type of society. This class seems to include most of our matrilineal-matrilateral societies (Class 3 above). In these societies, mother's brother's daughter marriage is, so to speak, over-determined: it is appropriate to the system of interpersonal relations, and it also satisfies the rule for succession to authority.

By symmetry in a four-fold table, in which we know the characteristics of three of the classes, we might in theory expect a fourth class, to wit:

D. *Patrilineages with amitalocal (uxorilocal) residence at marriage.* Murdock and Leach believe that societies truly of this class do not exist. Certainly our patrilineal-patrilateral societies (Class 2 above) do not belong to it, both being patrilineal-patrilocal. But we can state what characteristics such societies should have if they did exist, and in so stating understand why they do not. The continuing core of the local group should consist of *patrilineally-related women* (father's sisters and brother's daughters). The men of the lineage should move out, the men of other lineages should move in, at marriage. Authority should be transmitted from father to son, and on considerations of pure symmetry, without regard for the locus of jural authority, father's sister's daughter marriage should be the rule, if unilateral cross-cousin marriage took place at all.

Unhappily theoretical possibilities in this case run into practical difficulties. In a local group whose core was formed by patrilineally-related women, there would be a serious problem in following the rule of transmission of authority. It can be shown that, under the given conditions, unlike those of the matrilineal-matrilocal societies (Class C above), father-in-law cannot also be of the same lineage as son-in-law and of the same local group at the time of transmission of authority. Neither father's sister's daughter marriage nor mother's brother's daughter marriage would allow him to be both. Mother's brother's daughter marriage would allow ego after marriage to live in the same local group as his father, who would not, of course, be father-in-law too. But if ego, in his early years, resides with his father in almost all societies, then the local group that ego would be born into would also be the one he married into. He would be *already there.* Or if he moved out, like the Trobriand young man, before marriage, he would have to move back at marriage. Presumably authority would be transmitted from father to son, but this, taken together with the persistent association of each with the same local group, would have the tendency to turn such societies, if they ever existed, into patrilineal-patrilocal ones (Class A). If it ever came into being, the life-expectancy of a patrilineal-amitalocal society, as such, would be short. Interestingly enough, the theoretical requirements of a patrilineal-amitalocal society could be met if the marriage rule was that ego married father's sister's daughter who was also mother's brother's daughter. This would make the society one of Kariera type, which is effectively, as we should expect, patrilineal-patrilocal. These structural difficulties and instabilities go far to explain why societies of the patrilineal-amitalocal class do not seem to exist.

In this last section, we have tried to put our three largest classes (1, 3, and 4) of societies practicing unilateral cross-cousin marriage into a wider framework of types of social organization, and to show why our smallest class (patrilineal-patrilateral, Class 2) must be made up of real "sports." We know enough of the Sherente to see that they have a very unusual kind of social organization.

In the course of this examination, we have also had reason to remember Lévi-Strauss's statement that unilateral cross-cousin marriage of either kind would be found associated with what he called harmonic regimes.[79] We have no difficulty in agreeing that societies of classes A and C above are harmonic regimes in Lévi-Strauss's terms; they are patrilineal-patrilocal and matrilineal-matrilocal respectively, and when they practice unilateral cross-cousin marriage they adopt the matrilateral form. Whether the societies of class B, the matrilineal-avunculocal ones practicing the patrilateral form, are also harmonic in Lévi-Strauss's terms is not so clear. For him a regime is harmonic if "the rule of residence is the same as the rule of filiation."[80] We might argue that the Trobrianders have a harmonic regime because ego belongs to the same lineage as his mother's brother and goes to live with mother's brother when he grows up. We might also argue that the Trobrianders were matrilineal-patrilocal, in that ego belongs to the same lineage as his mother but certainly does not continue to live where she does. In short, what Lévi-Strauss means by either *residence* or *filiation* is not unambiguous enough to deal with the Trobriand case. We might also argue that no society in the world is effectively dysharmonic. In any event, Lévi-Strauss uses harmony and dysharmony to separate unilateral societies from bilateral ones. We are interested only in distinguishing between the two kinds of unilateral rules and have nothing to say about bilateral ones. Lévi-Strauss's further statement that the matrilateral rule depends only on the harmonic character of the regime and has nothing to do with linearity we have already shown to be correct only if we neglect to compare the *number* of patrilineal societies following the rule with the number of matrilineal ones. The rule is in fact heavily associated with patriliny.

Conclusion

Let us now sum up what we believe we have accomplished in this book.

We took our departure from a criticism of Lévi-Strauss's *Les structures élémentaires de la parenté,* using a study of the two forms of unilateral cross-cousin marriage as a test of his theory. In the place of two crucial statements of his, we adopted different hypotheses. These statements were: *a.* that the adoption of the matrilateral form (mother's brother's daughter marriage) had nothing to do with the linearity of a society, and *b.* that more societies would practice the matrilateral form than the patrilateral (father's sister's daughter marriage), because the former was better than the latter at creating organic solidarity in the society. We argued instead: *a.* that linearity was indeed a determinant and that the matrilateral form would tend to be found in patrilineal societies, the patrilateral in matrilineal ones (our special hypothesis), and *b.* that the "goodness" of the form (in Lévi-Strauss's sense) was not a determinant and that the choice of form would be determined by the locus of jural authority over ego and the consequent pattern of interpersonal relations among kinsmen (our general theory). We expected to find one locus and pattern in patrilineal societies, another in matrilineal ones. We then proceeded to test our hypotheses by a cross-cultural survey.

By means of this survey, we have shown a significant correlation between the linearity of societies and their rules of unilateral cross-cousin marriage. Mother's brother's daughter marriage is the rule in patrilineal societies, father's sister's daughter in matrilineal ones significantly more often than the matrilateral type in matrilineal societies, the patrilateral type in patrilineal ones. That is, we have produced evidence in favor of our special hypothesis. As far as our list of societies is concerned, we have shown that Lévi-Strauss was wrong in arguing that linearity had nothing to do with the form of unilateral cross-cousin marriage, but the discovery of a few more unilateral societies might conceivably upset our correlation.

In the course of examining other data on the societies on our list, we have shown a far more significant correlation between the locus of jural authority over ego and the rule of unilateral cross-cousin marriage. From our general theory we argued that, if the locus of jural authority over ego, before marriage, is his father, then, provided unilateral cross-cousin marriage is allowed at all, the matrilateral form will be the rule, and if the locus of jural authority over ego, before marriage, is his mother's brother, the patrilateral form will be the rule. Among those societies on our list for which we have evidence on the locus of authority, there is only one exception to this hypothesis—the Yir-Yoront—, though the Sherente conform to it only in part: father's sister's daughter marriage is the rule, and father is *not* the locus of jural authority over ego. It will take the discovery of many exceptional societies to upset this hypothesis.

We have also come to understand why our special hypothesis received less significant support than this more general one. In at least one formally patrilineal society—the Sherente—jural authority over ego is not vested in the father, and in several matrilineal societies—the matrilocal ones—authority is not vested in mother's brother but in father. If anyone wants to say that we, like Lévi-Strauss, are now arguing that linearity has nothing to do with unilateral cross-cousin marriage, we shall accept the criticism, provided he adds that we believe *potestality* has a great deal to do with it. Potestality is a far better predictor than linearity.

Our general theory did more than predict a relation between the locus of jural authority over ego and the form of unilateral cross-cousin marriage: it also explained why this relation should exist. It argued that the locus of jural authority in father or mother's brother would be an important determinant of ego's sentimental ties with kinsfolk. In the former case, father and father's sister would be sentimentally "distant" from ego, mother's brother "close." And in the latter case, mother's brother would be "distant," father and father's sister "close." Authority discourages intimacy, or "there is a separation made between jural relations and relations of personal attachment."[81] We further argued that ego would tend to seek as his wife the daughter of the member of the older generation, outside his nuclear family, with whom he had formed the closest attachment, and that that person in turn would have good sentimental reasons for giving the daughter to ego. Not only the locus of jural authority, but also, in all the societies on our list for which we have information on these matters, except always the Yir-Yoront, the interpersonal ties have been of the type predicted. We have produced evidence in favor of our general theory. If this paper has anything to add to anthropology, it is less its negative contribution—the criticism of Lévi-Strauss—than its positive one—further evidence that authority is an important determinant of social behavior, that jural ties tend to be segregated from affectionate ones, and that sentiment plays its part in marriage in primitive societies as well as in modern Western ones. None of these propositions is surprising, but none has received the emphasis it deserves.

Lévi-Strauss argues that mother's brother's daughter marriage occurs in more societies than does father's sister's daughter marriage because the former is "better" for a *society*, as creating a higher degree of organic solidarity. That is, he gives what we have called a *final-cause* type of explanation for the frequency of the matrilateral form. This form is indeed the more common, and we should give Lévi-Strauss full credit for being correct, did we not believe that it is more common, not for Lévi-Strauss's reasons, but rather because societies in which jural authority over ego is vested in father are more numerous than those in which it is vested in mother's brother. In the locus of authority and the personal, sentimental interests it precipitates we have provided an *efficient-cause* type of explanation. Note that the facts on which we have based our theory are just the ones to which Lévi-Strauss pays least attention. He has little to say about what we have called "interpersonal relations" and less about authority. We believe that the forces he exiled have returned to undo him, and that his model of social behavior is too formal and abstract.

More soberly, we do not argue that Lévi-Strauss's final cause theory is right or that it is wrong, but only that it is now unnecessary. We have been able to point out some of the other features of social systems and individual behavior that determine the adoption of the patrilateral or the matrilateral form of unilateral cross-cousin marriage, whether or not one is "better" than the other. Or, to put the matter another way, our theory will predict *what* societies will adopt *what* form, and Lévi-Strauss's theory will not. But remember that we have never claimed to specify all the determinants of the phenomena. For one thing, we have not tried to explain why some societies have a unilateral rule of either form and others do not. That is the next task, and a big one. We suspect empirically, without being able to explain why it should be the case, that unilateral cross-cousin marriage is especially likely to occur in societies where lineage is important but the number of members of any lineage living close together in the same place is small.

For obviously no theory will explain everything: something must always be accepted as given. In the case of our theory, a critic may well say: "Granted you have shown that matrilateral marriage occurs more often than patrilateral, not because it is better, but because there are more patripotestal societies than avuncupotestal ones. This latter fact remains to be explained; you have only shifted the issue to new ground, and a final cause theory may still be valid if *patria potestas* is in some sense better than *avunculi potestas.*" We should then argue, though we should not be able to prove our case, that it may indeed be better, but not necessarily in the sense of "better for a society as an organic whole." Consider the fact that in our list there are just twice as many patrilineal-patrilocal-patripostestal societies as all the others put together. These are societies the core of whose local groups consists of fathers and sons, generation after generation, and in which men need not leave their old homes either before or at marriage. If men are, in general, of higher status than women in all societies, and if the effectiveness of the men is increased by preserving from early childhood their association with the same hunting grounds or the same farm land, then the patrilineal-patrilocal-patripotestal organization may well be better than other forms of organization, as serving both social and economic interests. The organization is more convenient for the men and their local groups, and for this reason may be adopted more often than other forms. But this is very different from saying it is better for society as an organic whole. Pursuing their interests men create social structures, which then create new interests, and so on. Some of these structures may indeed turn out to be better for society as a whole than others, and thus indirectly serve the interests of individuals. But we doubt that the final cause alone is ever a sufficient condition for the existence of an institution.

NOTES

1. Paris, Presses Universitaires de France, 1949.
2. A. R. Radcliffe-Brown, *Structure and Function in Primitive Society* (Glencoe, Ill., Free Press, 1952), pp. 15-31. The paper was originally published in 1924.
3. A good summary of Lévi-Strauss's book, with some useful criticism, is J. P. B. de Josselin de Jong, *Lévi-Strauss's Theory on Kinship and Marriage* (*Mededelingen van het Rijksmuseum voor Volkenkunde, No. 10*), Leiden, Brill, 1952.
4. *Op. cit.*, p. 64.
5. *Ibid.*, p. 65.
6. One of the few examples is that of the Beduin and other groups influenced through Islam by Beduin custom.
7. *Op. cit.*, p. 274.
8. *Ibid.*, p. 270.
9. *Ibid.*, p. 271.
10. *Ibid.*, p. 548.
11. Paris, 1893, ch. III, sec. 4.
12. *Op. cit.*, p. 553.
13. *Ibid.*, p. 558.
14. E. R. Leach, "The Structural Implications of Matrilateral Cross-Cousin Marriage," *Journal of the Royal Anthropological Institute*, Vol. 81 (1951), pp. 23-55.
15. For a discussion of Malinowski's and Radcliffe-Brown's theories of magic, see G. C. Homans, *The Human Group* (New York, Harcourt, Brace, 1950), pp. 321-330.
16. A. R. Radcliffe-Brown, *Structure and Function in Primitive Society* (Glencoe, Ill., Free Press, 1952), p. 180.
17. Quoted in D. W. Thompson, *On Growth and Form* (New York, 1948), p. 6.
18. See R. B. Braithwaite, *Scientific Explanation* (Cambridge, Cambridge University Press, 1953), pp. 319-341.
19. *Op. cit.*, pp. 558-566.
20. See E. R. Leach, "The Structural Implications of Matrilateral Cross-Cousin Marriage," *Journal of the Royal Anthropological Institute*, Vol. 81 (1951), p. 53.
21. A. R. Radcliffe-Brown, *Structure and Function in Primitive Society* (Glencoe, Ill., Free Press, 1952), pp. 15-31.
22. R. Firth, *We, The Tikopia* (New York, 1936).
23. This is a Barnardian definition of authority. See C. I. Barnard, *The Functions of the Executive* (Cambridge, Mass., 1938), ch. XII.
24. For a discussion of jural relations, see A. R. Radcliffe-Brown, "Introduction," *African Systems of Kinship and Marriage*, A. R. Radcliffe-Brown and D. Forde, eds. (New York, 1950), p. 11.

25. I. Schapera, "Kinship and Marriage among the Tswana," *African Systems of Kinship and Marriage*, A. R. Radcliffe-Brown and D. Forde, eds. (New York, 1950), p. 142.

26. R. Firth, *We, the Tikopia* (New York, 1936), pp. 209-210; A. R. Radcliffe-Brown, "Introduction," *African Systems of Kinship and Marriage*, A. R. Radcliffe-Brown and D. Forde, eds., p. 26.

27. New York, Harcourt Brace, 1950, pp. 230-280.

28. G. G. Brown, "Hehe Cross-Cousin Marriage" in E. E. Evans-Pritchard, R. Firth, B. Malinowski, and I. Schapera, eds., *Essays Presented to C. G. Seligman* (London, 1934), p. 28.

29. *Ibid.*, p. 35.

30. *Op. cit.*, p. 531-535.

31. See especially B. Malinowski, *The Father in Primitive Psychology* (London, 1927) and *Sex and Repression in Savage Society* (London, 1927).

32. B. Malinowski, *The Sexual Life of Savages in North-Western Melanesia* (London, 1952), pp. 81, 450-451.

33. F. Eggan, *The Social Organization of the Western Pueblos* (Chicago, Chicago University Press, 1950), pp. 39-41; M. Titiev, "The Problem of Cross-Cousin Marriage among the Hopi," *American Anthropologist*, New Series, Vol. 40 (1938), pp. 105-111.

34. At a session of the anthropological section of the American Association for the Advancement of Science, 28 December 1951.

35. *Op. cit.*, pp. 332-333.

36. *Ibid.*, p. 334.

37. New York, Macmillan, 1949.

38. E. K. Gough, "Changing Kinship Usages in the Setting of Political and Economic Change among the Nayars of Malabar," *Journal of the Royal Anthropological Institute*, Vol. 82 (1952), pp. 73-74.

39. E. R. Leach, "The Structural Implications of Matrilateral Cross-Cousin Marriage," *Journal of the Royal Anthropological Institute*, Vol. 81 (1951), pp. 24-25.

40. J. C. Mitchell, *The Yao Village*, (unpublished ms.).

41. M. Fortes, "Kinship and Marriage among the Ashanti," in A. R. Radcliffe-Brown and D. Forde, eds., *African Systems of Kinship and Marriage* (New York, 1950), p. 279.

42. G. P. Murdock, "Kinship and Social Behavior among the Haida," *American Anthropologist*, New Series, Vol. 36 (1934), p. 364.

43. P. T. R. Gurdon, *The Khasis* (London, 1914), p. 78.

44. Our chief sources for these societies are those cited in G. P. Murdock, *Social Structure* (New York, Macmillan, 1949), plus the following: Altaians and Teleuts: N. P. Dryenkova, "Klassifikatsionnaya sistema i brachnye normy a altaitsev i teleut," in L. Ya. Shternberg, ed., *Sbornik materialov po svad'be i semeino-rodovoyu stroyu narodov S.S.S.R.* (Leningrad, 1926), Vol. 1.; Gilyak: L. Ya. Shternberg, *Sem'ia i rod* (Leningrad, 1933); Gold: O. Lattimore, *The Gold Tribe, "Fishskin Tatars"* of the

Lower Sungari (Memoirs of the American Anthropological Association, No. 40, 1933); Kachin: E. R. Leach, *The Political Systems of Highland Burma* (London, 1953); Karadjeri: A. P. Elkin, "Social Organization of the Kimberley Division, Northwestern Australia," *Oceania*, Vol. 2 (1932), pp. 296-333; Lovedu: E. J. Krige and J. D. Krige, *The Realm of a Rain-Queen* (London, 1943); Mbundu: G. M. Childs, *Umbundu Kinship and Character* (Oxford, Oxford University Press, 1949); Mende: K. L. Little, *The Mende of Sierra Leone* (London, 1951); Sandawe: O. Dempwolff, *Die Sandawe* (Hamburg, 1916); Wik-Munkan: U. McConnel, "The Wik-Munkan and Allied Tribes of the Cape York Peninsula, N.Q., Part III," *Oceania*, Vol. 4 (1934), pp. 310-367; Yir-Yoront: L. Sharp, "The Social Organization of the Yir-Yoront Tribe, Cape York Peninsula: Part I: Kinship and the Family," *Oceania*, Vol. 4 (1934), pp. 404-431; Kandyu: U. McConnel, "Social Organization of the Tribes of the Cape York Peninsula," *Oceania*, Vol. 10 (1940), pp. 434-455; Sherente: C. Nimuendajú, *The Serente*, trans. R. H. Lowie (Los Angeles, The Southwest Museum, 1942); Garo: A. Playfair, *The Garos* (London, 1909); Kaonde: F. H. Melland, *In Witch-Bound Africa* (London, 1923); Kaska: J. H. Honigmann, *Culture and Ethos of Kaska Society* (Yale University Publications in Anthropology, No. 40, New Haven, 1946); Siriono: A. R. Holmberg, *Nomads of the Long Bow: The Siriono of Eastern Bolivia* (Institute of Social Anthropology, Smithsonian Institution, Publication No. 7, Washington, 1950); Ila: A. I. Richards, "Some Types of Social Structure among the Central Bantu," in A. R. Radcliffe-Brown and D. Forde, eds., *African Systems of Kinship and Marriage* (New York, 1950), pp. 207-251; Tlingit: F. de Laguna, "Some Dynamic Forces in Tlingit Society," *Southwestern Journal of Anthropology*, Vol. 8 (1952), pp. 1-12. We have had to rely on friends for information from the Russian sources.

45. R. A. Fisher, *Statistical Methods for Research Workers* (10th ed., Edinburgh, Oliver and Boyd, 1946), 96 ff.

46. G. M. Childs, *Umbundu Kinship and Character* (Oxford, Oxford University Press, 1949), pp. 44-45.

47. E. J. Krige and J. D. Krige, *The Realm of a Rain-Queen* (London, 1943), pp. 70-84.

48. W. L. Warner, *A Black Civilization* (New York, 1937), p. 99.

49. K. L. Little, *The Mende of Sierra Leone* (London, 1951), p. 110.

50. A. R. Radcliffe-Brown, "Introduction," in A. R. Radcliffe-Brown and D. Forde, eds., *African Systems of Kinship and Marriage* (New York, 1950), p. 37.

51. L. Sharp, "The Social Organization of the Yir-Yoront Tribe, Cape York Peninsula. Part I: Kinship and the Family," *Oceania*, Vol. 4, (1934) p. 412.

52. *Ibid.*, p. 415.

53. *Ibid.*, p. 426.

54. G. P. Murdock, "Kinship and Social Behavior among the Haida," *American Anthropologist*, New Series, Vol. 36, (1934), pp. 363-364.

55. F. de Laguna, "Some Dynamic Forces in Tlingit Society," *Southwestern Journal of Anthropology*, Vol. 8 (1952), pp. 11-12.
56. A. B. Deacon, "Notes on Some Islands of the New Hebrides," *Journal of the Royal Anthropological Institute*, Vol. 59 (1929), p. 483.
57. E. W. Smith and A. M. Dale, *The Ila-Speaking Peoples of Northern Rhodesia* (London, 1920).
58. A. I. Richards, "Some Types of Social Structure among the Central Bantu," in A. R. Radcliffe-Brown and D. Forde, eds., *African Systems of Kinship and Marriage* (New York, 1950), p. 239.
59. E. W. Smith and A. M. Dale, *The Ila-Speaking Peoples of Northern Rhodesia* (London, 1920), Vol. 1, pp. 319-320.
60. F. H. Melland, *In Witch-Bound Africa* (London, 1923), pp. 62-63.
61. *Ibid.*, p. 57.
62. J. H. Honigmann, *Culture and Ethos of Kaska Society* (Yale University Publications in Anthropology, No. 40, New Haven, 1946), p. 131.
63. *Ibid.*, pp. 124-125.
64. *Ibid.*, p. 129.
65. A. R. Holmberg, *Nomads of the Long Bow: The Siriono of Eastern Bolivia* (Institute of Social Anthropology, Smithsonian Institution, Publication No. 7, Washington, 1950), pp. 54, 81-83.
66. *Ibid.*, pp. 49-57.
67. A. Playfair, *The Garos* (London, 1909); T. C. Hodson, "The Garo and Khasi Marriage Systems Contrasted," *Man in India*, Vol. 1 (1921), pp. 106-127; J. K. Bose, "The Nokrom System of the Garos of Assam," *Man*, Vol. 36 (1936), pp. 44-46.
68. Playfair, *op. cit.*, p. 64.
69. *Ibid.*, p. 73.
70. U. McConnel, "Social Organization of the Tribes of the Cape York Peninsula," *Oceania*, Vol. 10 (1940), pp. 437-438.
71. C. Nimuendaju, *The Serente*, trans. R. H. Lowie (Los Angeles, The Southwest Museum, 1942), pp. 16-22.
72. *Ibid.*, p. 12, italics ours.
73. *Ibid.*, p. 43.
74. *Ibid.*, p. 50.
75. *Ibid.*, p. 26.
76. *Ibid.*, pp. 57-58.
77. G. P. Murdock, *Social Structure* (New York, Macmillan, 1949), pp. 69-71.
78. E. R. Leach, "The Structural Implications of Matrilateral Cross-Cousin Marriage," *Journal of the Royal Anthropological Institute*, Vol. 81 (1951), pp. 24-25.
79. Lévi-Strauss, *op. cit.*, p. 274.
80. *Ibid.*, p. 271.
81. A. R. Radcliffe-Brown, "Introduction," in A. R. Radcliffe-Brown and D. Forde, eds., *African Systems of Kinship and Marriage* (New York, 1950), p. 78.